WORLD DEMAND
FOR RAW MATERIALS
IN 1985 AND 2000

World Demand For Raw Materials In 1985 And 2000

Wilfred Malenbaum

Professor of Economics
University of Pennsylvania

E/MJ MINING INFORMATIONAL SERVICES
McGraw-Hill, Inc.
1221 Avenue of the Americas, New York, N.Y. 10020 U.S.A.

Library of Congress Catalog Card Number 78-10538
0-07-039789-9

Acknowledgement

This study was prepared with the support of the National Science Foundation Research Applied to National Needs Program Grant No. 75-23687. Outstanding contributions to the underlying statistical analysis were made by Jonathan A. Blau, Dal Hee Lee and Sheldon R. Stoughton, three of the university students who participated in the research program.

With minor editorial changes, the book is the report submitted under the NSF Grant. In particular, basic data used in the analysis were those available before September 1, 1977.

Any opinions, findings, conclusions or recommendations expressed in the publication are those of the author and do not necessarily reflect the views of the National Science Foundation.

Wilfred Malenbaum
Professor of Economics
University of Pennsylvania
Principal Investigator
NSF Grant No. 75-23687

TABLE OF CONTENTS

LIST OF TABLES:text

LIST OF TABLES: APPENDIX

Foreword
Major Conclusions

This Report presents new estimates of world demand for industrial raw materials in 1985 and in 2000. Changes to be anticipated in the level of total materials demand and in its distribution among world regions are relevant not only to the world minerals industry; these changes have an important role in policy and program with respect to international trade and investment, to the course of economic expansion in the industrialized lands, and to the modernization and growth of the world's poor nations. All these are currently matters of major concern in national and international affairs. While the present work does not address these policy issues, its provision of new data and its explanation of their derivation provide knowledge that will benefit policy formulation and implementation.

Annual rates of growth of demand for industrial raw materials differ among materials and among regions of the world. Yet there are systematic forces that cut across demand behavior by region and by raw material. These consistencies are critical to the process of future demand estimation and to the statistical results. Process as well as numbers are revealing with regard to alternative policy and program formulations.

The major conclusions in this Foreword involve statistics for raw materials as a group and material demand for the world as a whole and in two separate subcategories, U.S. and non-U.S. world, rich nations and poor nations. Specific materials and smaller regions are noted in the Foreword only where contrasts are relevant to major conclusions. Complete detail by region, time, and material is available in the text tables of the Report and Appendix.

Rates of Growth of Demand for Raw Materials

Over the years 1951-75, annual rates of growth of demand for materials in the world were high, often 5 percent and above; they tended to be higher than growth rates of total output of all final goods and services. Rates of growth of materials demand in the non-U.S. world were consistently above world rates. The non-U.S. rates exceeded U.S. rates by some 50 percent for aluminum and by 100-200 percent (occasionally more) for other materials. Poor nations had growth rates of demand that were often twice the level in rich nations. Japan, U.S.S.R., Eastern Europe also had annual growth rates above the average for the non-U.S. world; their growth rates of demand began to decline during the 1965-75 decade.

The U.S. share of total world materials use more or less halved from 1950 to 1975; the non-U.S. world share increased from some 50-60 percent of the total to about 75 percent. Non-U.S. rich nations expanded their share but at progressively slower rates over the 1951-75 period. By 1975, poor nations used 10 percent and more of total world materials, as against 5 percent and less in 1950.

A tendency toward declining rates of growth of world demand for all raw materials studied is manifest in the course of the 1951-1975 years. This tendency is expected to persist over future decades. For most raw materials, this will pertain in major subdivisions of the world and indeed in its regional components separately. Declines will be manifest by 1985 and further by 2000. The extent of decline and the time pattern will vary by material and by region. In particular, rapid declines in growth rates of materials demand in poor lands may moderate in some degree over the longer time interval. The poor nation share of total world use will continue to grow, albeit slowly.

It is useful to visualize the outlook for materials demand in terms of the outlook for its two components: intensity-of-use (I-U) of materials and total output of final goods and services (GDP).

Patterns of Change in Intensity-of-Use of Raw Materials

The intensity-of-use (I-U) of most materials and in world regions where most of each material is used has been declining over recent decades. A notable exception is aluminum: its I-U shows declining rates of increase. These patterns for the world are clearly manifest in rich nations. They are less definitive in the poor nations.

The forces responsible for the declining pattern of intensity are:

(1) Shifts in the types of final goods and services that world consumers and investors demand directly;

(2) Technological developments that alter the efficiency with which raw materials are discovered, extracted, processed, distributed and utilized in production of final goods; and

(3) Substitutions among raw materials inputs consequent upon relative price movements and relative rates of technological development.

For most materials world I-U will by 1985 be 5-10 percent below recent levels, and 10-20 percent below by 2000. These declines tend to continue I-U reductions initiated during or prior to the 1951-1975 time interval. Aluminum provides the only case of expanding intensity arising from forces of substitution. The aluminum I-U showed average annual increases of 3.8, 4.7, 4.3, and 2.3 percent over successive five-year intervals in the past. Comparable increases are projected at 0.8 and 0.7 percent to 1985 and 2000, respectively.

The projected I-U levels reflect the evidence of the persistence of patterns associated with the three causal forces listed. In particular, the technological development force is now expected to have an expanding impact on I-U in poor nations. I-U changes attributable to technology may parallel those in the rich nations in briefer time interval than was anticipated in earlier research.

The I-U evidence constitutes strong support for the argument that man's knowledge, skill and aspirations have served to slacken his need for industrial raw materials. Such a *demand* prospect counters the growth-limiting significance often attributed to the inelastic nature of raw materials *supply*. Through market price and public policy responses, such supply characteristics may also stimulate the forces that lower I-U.

Rates of Growth of Total Output of Final Goods and Services

The world's annual rates of GDP growth over the periods to 1985 and 2000 are expected to average 25-30 percent below their 1951-1975 annual rates. With the rates of population growth anticipated by the U.N. Population Office, world per capita GDP will grow over the next decades at average rates at least 40 percent below their 1951-1975 growth levels. Nonetheless, in absolute terms, real per capita GDP for the world will exceed 1971-1975 levels by some 20 percent in 1985 and some 50 percent in 2000. Important changes are not anticipated in relative GDP growth among component regions of the world. Significant shifts in relative GDP levels or relative GDP per capita levels among these regions are thus considered unlikely.

The fundamental explanation for this outlook in GDP growth is the critical role in future economic progress of such goals as more equitable national income distribution, reduced unemployment and underemployment, and higher relative productivity in present low-income sectors, i.e., agriculture, other rural production, many public sector activities. Current policies and programs for progress in GDP continue to focus on fiscal and monetary tools, on transfers of goods and knowledge from rich to poor nations. The development results of the past 10-15 years emphasize the need for new policy and new action to achieve a broad base of participation in economic change by the vast bulk of the populations in each world region.

New development doctrine is still evolving; leadership commitment cannot occur soon. The impressive world growth performance of 1951-1975 notwithstanding, the outlook for 1985 and even for 2000 is significantly lower annual average world GDP growth rates than prevailed in 1951-1975.

Factors Underlying Materials Demand Growth

Annual growth rates of world demand for many materials over the next few decades are seen to be 40-60 percent of the levels prevailing during 1951-1975. This is due to the orders of magnitude of change anticipated in I-U levels and in GDP growth rates. Marked declines in rates of demand growth will occur in rich, non-U.S. nations. In general, their I-U levels are approaching the low levels already attained in the U.S.; their average GDP growth rates are declining from 1951-1975 levels significantly above those in the U.S.

The reduced rates of growth of materials demand are attributable more to the future rates of GDP growth than to the lower levels of I-U in future years. Perhaps 60-70 percent of the reduction arises from the GDP component, the rest from the I-U component. The former is influenced by forces that national policies will seek to alter: a high rate of GDP growth is a popular goal throughout the world. In important measure, its achievement rests on the actions a nation takes to achieve economic progress. The I-U component embodies fundamental and persistent forces for continuous and perhaps more marked decline.

The fundamental elements of I-U change are the desires, aspirations and skills of man. The record of I-U decline is an account of human capacity to reconcile the scale and pattern of raw materials use and of final goods demand with the realities of world resource endowments. This human capacity can also serve to sustain progress in GDP growth rates. The I-U record and prospect provide some assurance that higher GDP growth rates can occur even as I-U levels continue to decline.

Some Consequences of Demand Growth Patterns

The outlook for materials demand growth rates indicates that materials supply growth rates will also be reduced by some 40-60 percent over the period to 2000. Slower growth rates of materials demand in rich lands will tend to affect the relative growth rate of foreign trade in these materials. The current study does not permit any straightforward generalization as to possible changes in im-

3

port rates or import levels in the different regions of the world. On the whole however, the foreign markets for raw materials produced in the poor nations will tend to expand relatively faster among the poor nations themselves.

The overall outlook for future demand and supply forces for materials suggests a gradual weakening of demand forces relative to supply forces: the long-term tendency, to 1985 and to 2000, may thus be for lower materials prices relative to prices of the final products in which they are used.

Further Research Directions

The intensity-of-use concept provides intellectual and operational devices for analysis of supply and demand forces bearing on materials input, including their future prospects. The longer time interval and the extended list of raw materials included in the current research study have established greater certainty than existed only a few years back with respect to the shape of I-U patterns. The new work has strengthened the hypothesis that declines in I-U with growth of per capita GDP reflect man's capacity to discover ever broader ranges of alternative methods to fill a widening range of alternative and expanding needs. Future GDP potential rests on considerations relevant to the *quality of man* rather than to the *quantity of material.*

Further work on the quantitative determinants of I-U change may help to focus additional efforts of man to further progress. The current research made some inroads on this subject by identifying the role of technological change vis-a-vis the role of structural change in the economy and by conceptualizing the analytical separation of I-U between techniques and structure. The research can be carried further productively. Additional study of differences among nations in a material's I-U at any time point and in individual nations or regions over time periods may yield quantitative guides to specific policy tools in the materials area. Both direction of I-U movement and rate of change of I-U level differ for regions and for materials. In this diversity may lie meeting grounds in current controversy on policy and programs for efficient use of raw materials in the different parts of the world. Large benefits for the world and its regions can accrue from additional research on the factors that determine the world's need for industrial raw materials.

Chapter I
Introduction

This study is an analysis of the future demand for the following minerals and metals that are important inputs for industrial output throughout the world: aluminum, chrome, cobalt, copper, iron, manganese, nickel, platinum, steel, tin, tungsten and zinc. Together they account for 80-90 percent of the value of world mineral production. Total world demand for each of these twelve materials has increased significantly over the two decades from 1951-1955 through 1971-1975. Increases of about 100 percent were recorded in one or two cases, of 200 to 300 percent in most cases, and of as much as 400 or 500 percent in a few cases.

Utilization of these inputs is concentrated in the world's rich industrialized nations. With less than 30 percent of total world population, these countries account for over 80 percent of total world use of most of these twelve materials. In these lands, important components of materials consumption are imported. Thus, the United States depends upon imports for all its consumption of three or four of these materials and for at least 50 percent of total consumption in the case of four or five more. Other rich lands, Japan and West Germany in particular, are even more dependent on imported ores or metals for their raw materials consumption than is the United States.

Over the past few years, the world has been alerted to the reality of "limits to growth," due in important measure to recognition of the finite dimensions of the earth's nonrenewable minerals resources. Can utilization of these raw materials continue to expand at rates of recent decades? Minerals resources endowment and consumption are, of course, not matched country by country or even world region by region. Will world trade in ores, metals and minerals continue to distribute world supplies so as to meet the materials needs in individual countries and regions? In particular, there is large concentration of some resources in nations that are at early stages of modernization and industrialization. For example, almost 40 percent of the world's copper production and some 75 percent of its tin production are in developing lands. Will changing relationships between supply and demand for raw materials result in significant shifts in the distribution of world income flows?

Such questions are of major concern to private and public interests throughout the world, and they appear on the agenda of current international discussions. They place a premium upon analysis of the future outlook for raw materials that are important to the output of modern industry, transport or power.

This study focuses on the outlook for world *demand* in some future year less than a decade hence, in 1985, and in a generation or so, in the year 2000. The study has two specific and interrelated goals:

(1) to provide realistic estimates of demand for these twelve materials in the two future periods for the world, and for the ten component regions into which the world is here divided; and

(2) to contribute to methodology for such projections through application of what is called "intensity-of-use" procedures.

The emphasis here is upon demand, and not directly upon supply or trade. It is with respect to world demand that there exists an important knowledge gap. Demand projections for important minerals are often made for the United States and in smaller measure for a few other major consuming nations. Systematic study has not been devoted to the regions of the world where past use has been relatively small, but where potential demand may experience dynamic future expansion. In these regions, the outlook for supply and trade as well as for demand has great relevance for policy and action in the years ahead.

The less developed nations of the world have certainly been stimulated and encouraged by the dramatic success of the OPEC lands in achieving rapid expansion in their national product and especially in their percentage claims on total world product. Why not parallel achievement through other important industrial inputs? The world did in fact experience a phenomenal price increase in nonfuel minerals over the 1971-1974 years. It is true that this was followed by a precipitous price decline in most industrial raw materials from mid-1974 to late 1975. For some important raw materials, relative prices have continued to decline in the late 1970s. Yet the possibilities of limited expansion of world supply along with vistas of expanding world economic growth nourish poor nation expectations of high materials demand and increased relative prices. Whatever is the best economic judgment on such expectations, it is true today that these nations see relative economic gains through the ores and materials route. U.N. organizations, with membership dominated by poor lands, foresee an enhanced status from the economic prospects of net exporters of industrial raw materials.

The world is now heavily involved in international discussions on the economic power of ores, minerals and other raw materials. Under U.N. pressures the U.S. may already have adopted a different and more favorable stance on international commodity agreements than it had earlier maintained. The "commodity" role in poor nation growth has assumed a political status with respect to third-world development earlier preempted by foreign assistance. However unique the petroleum position among raw materials, however limited the prospect for sharp relative differentials in the price increases of nonfuel and nonagricultural raw materials, the world can now anticipate years in which supply and demand decisions with regard to key industrial inputs will involve not market forces alone but also major international efforts on the part of public organizations, national and multinational. What materials the world will need and how this total need will be distributed in different nations promise to remain matters of persistent public concern at both national and international levels.

Study of materials demand involves questions of relative price developments for materials inputs as well as for the output of the final goods and services in which inputs are used, and indeed for alternative materials that may be substitutable in alternative final goods production. Demand estimates for any future year for the world's component regions thus reflect judgments on supply and trade developments. Realistic demand estimates constitute important points of assessment for conventional projections of materials supply and its international movement.

A final point with respect to the importance of demand projections is that they permit, indeed they require, clarification on the *dependence of national product upon materials inputs* as against *a causal sequence from national product to materials inputs*. The present study had to deal with this circle; the arguments on this matter are relevant to current concerns of international development policy and program with regard to raw materials, (Chapter II).

As regards intensity-of-use analysis, the present study provides strong support for the relevance of its procedures in deriving estimates of future demand for materials, including estimates for regions of the world with limited economic data. Comprehensive and systematic projections also turn out to be revealing with respect to "laws of demand" for intermediate inputs, where demand is derived and not primary. Preliminary analysis using this method in the recent past has already contributed new understanding of the dynamics of the current world materials position. Of particular note is the evidence of increases in use intensities in poor lands along with decreases in intensities in the rich lands. Such offsetting tendencies provide new insight for projections of future materials demand in the world as a whole.

It is also clear from past studies that the rates of growth in the use of industrial raw materials in the world's poor nations have led the expansion in materials use in the whole world over the decades from 1950. As noted above, the volume of minerals used up in the world has multiplied since that time. The growth rate of demand has been more rapid in all world regions outside the United States. In particular, the most rapid rates of growth in consumption were in the world's poor nations as a group. This is indicated by the following data from a 1973 study (Table 1a):

Table 1a
Growth Rates of Materials Consumption: 1951-69
(Annual Average Percent)

	U.S.	World	Poor Nations
Steel	2.7	6.2	8.2
Iron Ore	1.6	6.2	14.4
Copper	2.5	4.7	7.6
Aluminum	7.4	9.2	17.8
Zinc	2.3	4.9	12.1
Sulfur	3.5	5.6	15.1
Total Energy	4.6	4.8	8.4

The poor nation share of the greatly enlarged total of world use more than doubled from less than 5 percent in 1950 to over 10 percent by the late 1960s. The specific increases are, of course, different for each raw material. Broadly, the U.S. share of total world use actually declined.

The import component of United States use of ores and minerals has been increasing. In 1970, some 15 percent of all U.S. consumption of the listed materials came from abroad as against an average of about 10 percent in 1950. More than one-third of these imports now originates in the poor nations. Other rich industrial countries, notably Japan and Western Europe, import four-fifths of these input materials. They depend more heavily upon the poor nations for them than does the United States.

Since these materials are used up by man as he generates the power, the transport, and the national product he desires, the demand for such inputs tends to be income-elastic. This is particularly so where national policy emphasizes modernization, as in low income economies dominated by agriculture and by extractive industries. Below are income elasticities of demand for important industrial raw materials over a recent period. Poor nation elasticities tend to be above those in most rich lands, although only the high income U.S. economy had income elasticities significantly below unity.[1] The high elasticities in the developing lands reflect both the new dynamism in the growth of traditional economies over these years and the new types of industrial outputs associated with that process. In any event, these elasticity measures are testimony of the differential pattern of materials demand growth in the less developed regions of the world. Incomes were expanding; their populations, already above 70 percent of the total, constitute an increasing share of the world.

Table 1b
Income Elasticities of Demand: 1951-55/1966-69

	Iron Ore	Aluminum	Zinc
Africa	14.02	15.89	5.61
Asia	2.39	13.52	4.54
Latin America	5.09	4.87	1.89
Mainland China	10.90	53.50	19.29
Western Europe	1.26	2.38	0.82
Japan	5.04	4.70	1.64
U.S.A.	0.38	2.60	0.58

Note has already been made of the new economic outlook in the international posture of the world's poor nations.

The present study is a further step in the materials demand analysis previously undertaken by the author. In a 1973 report,[2] demand estimates were

---

[1]Aluminum is an important exception (below, pp. 54-57).

[2]*Materials Requirements in the United States and Abroad in the Year 2000,* prepared for the National Commission on Materials Policy, Washington, D.C., March 1973. It is now available through National Technical Information Service, Springfield, Virginia 22151, as PB 219-675/PB (hereafter *NCMP 1973*).

presented for a number of raw materials in the year 2000, separately for each of ten component regions of the world. These regional results were also combined on a total world basis and on a total non-U.S. world basis. Tables 1a and 1b above were derived from this study. For the present work, crude steel, iron ore, refined copper, primary aluminum and zinc were reexamined. Fluorspar and sulfur have been omitted, as have total energy and all the energy components specifically projected in the 1973 study (solid fuels, liquid fuels, natural gas, other energy sources). The additional materials included here, specifically chrome, cobalt, manganese, nickel, platinum, tin and tungsten, posed major data problems. In some measure, this is because some of these materials are traded internationally in diverse forms. Only partial efforts seem to have been made earlier to assemble homogeneous data on a world basis. Preliminary solutions have been derived here. Relevant demand estimates are presented for twelve separate materials, the five considered earlier and these additional seven metals. Again, the answers are for individual regions, with a total world and non-U.S. world, as well as totals for the rich nations and for the poor nations of the world. All data are now available for 1985 as well as 2000.

Where there is overlap (five raw materials, as projected to 2000), the two studies have the same thrust: total materials requirements grow rapidly to multiples of the levels in the early 1970s. But the future estimates here are appreciably below those of the 1973 report. Two factors are responsible for this change in the level of two sets of estimates prepared by the same research group within a short time interval. Fundamental is the evidence now available on intensity-of-use. There can be no doubt of the strength of the forces making for reductions in this parameter with more rapid rates of decline than were foreseen in the early work. Moreover, the poor-nation component now offers less counter within this overall decline than was reflected in that work. Technological advances are adopted readily, even at relatively low levels of GDP per person (Chapter IV below).

The new evidence on use-intensities may of course reflect in some measure the views on basic materials scarcities that had vogue in the early 1970s, and after the *NCMP 1973* estimates were made. The limits idea undoubtedly encouraged man and society to confront the shortage prospect with more intensive materials use. The history of materials use makes clear that adaptation serves to reduce the relative weight and relative cost of primary inputs into man's production of final goods and services. Since demand for inputs is a derived demand, final goods demanded *directly* tend to be given forms that minimize outlays on intermediate products whenever changes to that end are technologically possible and economically justifiable.

The materials evidence assembled and analyzed for this study lend support to this historic theme. High levels of economic progress can be maintained even while growth rates of materials inputs fall significantly below the rates of use of recent decades.

The other factor responsible for lower projections of materials demand is a set of new and lower projections of GDP growth essentially throughout the world. In the early 1970s when the original study was in progress, careful appraisal already prompted GDP growth projections in *NCMP 1973* well below those of the 1951-69 period, in some contrast to projections in other studies undertaken at that time.[3] But the internal structure of world economic decline since 1973 has provided strong additional evidence on the nature of the forces needed for high

---

[3]Thus see the collection of such projections assembled by the National Academy of Sciences and presented as Appendix to Section IV in its *Mineral Resources and the Environment*, Washington, D.C., February 1975.

rates of economic expansion. The present study's appraisals of the new growth theory as well as its analysis of the actual growth experience since 1950 prompted the determination to apply generally lower average GDP growth rates over the next decades. These lower rates are not reflections of materials shortages. On the contrary, they are expected to prevail despite persistent underuse of the world potential for economic output. The specific outlook for world GDP in the present Report is given below (Chapter III).

The systematic and comprehensive estimates of materials demand in *NCMP 1973* were a unique set: they were indeed "first estimates" without comparable alternatives. The published Report stressed the preliminary nature of the results and the need for further and continuing study of materials use in order to extend an area of knowledge that could serve man and society everywhere. The present Report remains preliminary. It provides improved future estimates, and it provides corroboration of the usefulness of a basic methodology applied to a broader range of materials. But there remain further and additional tasks to pursue, particularly with respect to the specific causes of differences in intensity-of-use measures over time and among regions. Raw materials seem destined to play an important role in world economic programs; the intensity-of-use concept is relevant to future economic growth problems throughout the world. Given these expectations, it is hoped the present study will stimulate further investigations in the raw materials areas.

Chapter II
The Research Scheme

What factors determine the quantity of any specific industrial raw material a nation will use up over a given year? Given the need for answers for future time periods, these factors must themselves permit more straightforward and justifiable extrapolations than would the dependent variable (the amount of raw material used up) itself. Three factors were selected here as the best determining variables. Thus to estimate $_iD_t$, the use of material i in the year t, there is need for (1) the total value of final goods and services produced in the year t by a nation's endowments (GDP_t); (2) the nation's population in that year (p_t); and (3) what may be called the intensity-of-use of i in year t ($_iI\text{-}U_t$) defined so:

$$_iI\text{-}U_t = \frac{_iD_t}{GDP_t}$$

Obviously, $_iD_t \equiv (GDP_t) \bullet (_iI\text{-}U_t) = GDP_t \bullet \dfrac{_iD_t}{GDP_t}$

Following is a discussion of the nature of each factor's relationship to $_iD_t$ and of the interrelationships among the three factors. In particular, the discussion examines the relevance of a tautological formula in integrating the three factors to yield $_iD_t$.

1. *GDP_t*. Raw materials are intermediate-type inputs in the production process. Therefore, "using up" a raw material, i in t, can only mean its use in producing a nation's *final* goods and services during t. Ordinarily there is essentially no demand for i as end-product in itself; even inventory demand for carryovers of i reflects a time dimension of the same derived demand as the demand for i's current use in final goods. Hence, some measure of total national product, i.e., the value of all final goods and services produced by a nation's productive resources over a year's period, must be an important factor determining materials use. While there are arguments in favor of some *net* rather than gross measure of this product, the latter is used here. In any event, the GDP measure has greater statistical reliability and much broader availability than does any net measure. A negative consideration is the possible distortion of the intensity-of-use measure in periods of heavy stockpiling activity associated with marked price changes of some raw materials. This is revealed in actual data (e.g., in Japan in the early 1970s). Such inventory changes are often mat-

ters of record, and their distortions on the intensity measure can usually be taken into account (below, p. 32 for example).

Most projection schemes for materials demand do use this association with GDP. One can examine past relationships in this regard: *ex post*, the direction of determination may not be relevant, but not so for the *ex ante* purpose of prime concern here. For we use estimated GDP_{1985} or GDP_{2000} as one key determinant of $_iD$ in each of these two years. If material i is itself a significant determinant of GDP, the argument is circular and probably invalid. Currently, limits-to-growth themes have some vogue, although probably less so than was the situation in 1972 and 1973. The present study does not accept the view that GDP_t for t over a long period of years will be determined by the availability of any material i. Rather it argues (Chapter III below) that for such future t's GDP_t levels will be primarily the consequence of decisions and actions of man, whatever the availability of specific materials. Both theoretical and empirical considerations prompt this view, and these considerations were basic in the quantitative GDP growth projections presented in this report.

The first determining factor then will be each regional unit's level of national product, usually as GDP_t. And in the nature of materials use, one can hypothesize that upward GDP movement, other factors constant, will contribute to upward $_iD_t$ movement.

Given the goal of projecting $_iD_t$ for a range of i's, it may be noted here that in the formula, GDP_t is the same, whatever i. This constancy contributes an element of consistency in the twelve i's of this study as projections are made for future t's, i.e., for 1985 and 2000.

2. *Population* (p_t). The population role in $_iD$ is very different from the role of GDP; on the whole, the relationship of population change to $_iD$ is more complex than is the role of GDP. Nonetheless, many projections of $_iD_t$ do assume a positive population role, essentially parallel to the positive GDP role.[4]. It is obvious that a very wide gap persists between population shares and resources use shares. Thus, at mid-century the rich world, with less than one-third of the world's population used about 95 percent of the raw materials. The poor world ratio of materials use did move up dramatically between 1950 and 1970. But this was due not to their population growth but to their GDP growth. Despite the rapid population growth in these lands, GDP growth rates over those decades were still higher. Indeed, a relevant determining element turns out to be GDP/population, so that the relationship between changes in materials use and population change is usually *inverse*. This relationship is best discussed in connection with the third factor basic to $_iD_t$ determination in the present study.

3. *Intensity-of-Use* ($_iI$-U_t). This measures the physical amount of i used up per unit of GDP in any particular period. Comparisons among countries make it necessary to present GDP magnitudes in a single currency (U.S. $ here); comparisons over time require a constant price level (1971 here). Both the population factor and the intensity measure serve as correctives in the GDP contribution to estimates of $_iD_t$. "Population" corrects for the new number of people sharing a GDP level at time t. "Intensity" adjusts for the new structure of GDP as its product composition differs at a t level, and as new technology and new

---

[4]For example, two important and significant forecast studies, one by the U.S. Bureau of Mines (*Mineral Facts and Problems*, 1970, GPO, Washington, D.C.), and the other by Resources for the Future (*Population, Resources and the Environment: A Report to the U.S. Commission on Population Growth and the American Future*, R.G. Ridker, ed., GPO, Washington, 1972) seem to assume cumulative positive relationships for these two independent variables: $_iD$ increases when GDP or population increases. This is shown explicitly in summary results presented by D.B: Brooks and P.W. Andrews, "Mineral Resources, Economic Growth and World Population," *Science*, 5 July 1974, p. 15.

cost structures alter the process of GDP creation. The application of the intensity ratio in the study of materials use has begun to be explored only in very recent years.[5] Perhaps the present effort is the most comprehensive. As the discussion in Chapter IV makes clear, there is an analytic case for further and continuing research exploration of the relationship between physical inputs of intermediate materials and the real value of final goods and services.

Several aspects of this I-U measure are noteworthy. First, it is readily available over past years, given statistics on a nation's use of i. Second, the very concept of an input and output relationship has a technological dimension. It must reflect changes in use and efficiency of inputs to yield outputs, with account taken of changes in techniques (for input or output) and changes in market relationships associated with supply, demand and public policy bearing on inputs and outputs. Third, and of particular interest, the historical evidence on use-intensity suggests there are patterns of behavior of the measure. And these patterns may be identified with underlying theory and empirical time observation. Indeed, it is this systematic behavior of this measure that constitutes the big promise for its usefulness in demand analysis for raw materials.

Among the observed patterns are those that emerge when intensity-of-use in a region is associated with per capita GDP over a period of years. With such a relationship our tautological "formula," $_iD_t \equiv GDP_t \times (_iD_t \div GDP_t)$, incorporates all three of the determining factors considered here. There is of course a significant body of facts and of theory on the subject of the growth of nations. While theory and policy on this matter are today in some state of controversy, national growth does constitute an area central to the social science professions. Quite separate from this doctrine on GDP, the second term (the ratio that measures intensity-of-use) may well have significance beyond what its numerator and denominator have separately. Intensity-of-use could thus have an empirical and theoretical life of its own. In this event, the tautology converts into a useful analytic tool.

This is the context in which the present research scheme rests upon the identity formulation: changes in the three determining factors can be related to changes in levels of materials use.

As indicated in the Introduction, attention will be given to the following materials, ferrous and nonferrous in turn, and numbered as they appear in tabular presentations and discussions:

1. crude steel
2. iron ore
3. nickel
4. manganese ore
5. chrome ore
6. cobalt
7. tungsten
8. copper
9. aluminum
10. platinum-group
11. zinc
12. tin

Again as in the 1973 report, analysis will continue to consider the world in ten subdivisions, with subtotals (1) for the U.S. and non-U.S. regions, and again (2) for rich nations and poor nations. This "regionalization," actually more functional than geographic, represents an effort to differentiate within these large two world subdivisions. Each of the ten groups is considered to have a high enough degree of homogeneity to justify common assumptions with respect to changes in intensity-of-use of raw materials and in rates of total economic growth. Where individual country patterns reflect significant differences, some supplementary study was undertaken. While for some materials (nickel and the platinum-group, for example) data availability required some regional changes

---

[5]See the observations on this point in Brooks and Andrews, *ibid.*, pp. 15-16.

in the analysis (and this is of course evident in the text), there was no analytic reason to adopt alternative subcategorization in the present study. The major use centers for materials are treated as single regions (U.S., Japan, U.S.S.R., for example), or as regionally unified totals of countries (Western Europe, Eastern Europe). Similarly, common use behavior patterns were presumed to prevail in the large regions of developing, poor lands. Consideration of ten "regions" as against a larger number undoubtedly cost some detail in the results, but the study justifies the belief that use of a 10-region world did not introduce arbitrary elements in the demand projections.

These regions are defined as follows, again with number designations for textual presentation:

1. Western Europe—OECD countries in Europe
2. Japan
3. Other Developed Lands—Australia, Canada, Israel, New Zealand, South Africa
4. Union of Soviet Socialist Republics
5. Eastern European Countries—Soviet Bloc countries plus Albania, Yugoslavia
6. Africa—minus South Africa
7. Asia—minus Israel, Japan, Mainland China and related areas
8. Latin America
9. China—plus Mongolia, North Korea, North Vietnam
10. United States—plus Puerto Rico and overseas islands
11. *World*—Sum 1-10
12. *Non-U.S. World*—Sum 1-9
13. *Poor Nations*—Sum 6-9
14. *Rich Nations*—Sum 1-5, 10

Before presenting specific estimates for GDP and GDP/population in 1985 and 2000, and for $_iD_t \div GDP_t$ for each i in those years, some observations are made on the procedures employed. In all these measures, the historical record was initially assembled from 1951 to 1975 and where available from 1934-1938. Essentially all national product data and all population data were taken from United Nations sources. The output was converted to U.S. dollars in 1971 prices on the basis of exchange rate data. GDP estimates are from other sources only for areas and periods not reported by the United Nations. For the U.S.S.R. and for Mainland China, for which official data are not conceptually comparable with much of the remaining world, the adjusted figures prepared by specialist groups were used. Specifically, for the U.S.S.R., the gross product data are from reports prepared for the Joint Economic Committee of the U.S. Congress over the past decade; for China the same source has publications at least from 1972. For the most part, the historical record was interpreted on the basis of five-year averages, with recourse to individual years only to trace patterns of marked change within a five-year period, a problem that arose especially for regions composed of different countries not usually analyzed as a single unit, e.g., "Other Developed Lands."

On the population front, the U.N. data were the primary source of the figures through 1975 that are presented in the present study.

The basic historical tables on GDP and GDP per person, more or less to date, are thus these five-year averages in 1971 U.S. dollars. Again, they provide the available factual record. Projections for 1985 and 2000 were made *entirely* by estimating two *average* growth rates for GDP, one for the ten-plus years from the 1971-75 average to 1985, and the other for the 25-plus years from 1971-75 to 2000. While an important consideration in these estimated growth rates for GDP was the record of growth rates of past years, the basic factor was the expectation derived from underlying doctrine on economic expansion. With respect to population growth to 1985 and to 2000, reliance was placed (in 1977) on the most recent working papers of the Population Division of the United Nations Secretariat.[6] The GDP/population estimates for 1985 and 2000 were then derived.

The 1985 and the 2000 statistics are *not* statistical extrapolations. One could perhaps argue that modern nations have the knowledge and the capacity to generate higher GDP growth rates than they had a generation or so back. The evidence from 1951 does not reveal that these potentials have become realities, nor is there strong basis today for arguing that such knowledge and capacity will assure higher rates in the future. Thus, in only two of the ten regions was the average growth rate for 1966-1975 higher than for 1951-1960. In any event, the record for most regions shows significant year-to-year variations. Moreover, there is an increasing appreciation that the determinant forces for growth lie in the aspirations and commitment to economic expansion on the part of public and private leaders, much more than in resource endowment and supply and in technology. On the one hand, this analytic view plays down the role of materials limits to growth, and thus enhances the prospect for future progress. On the other hand, this view stresses the role of leadership and its determination to cope with whatever deterrents impede achievement of a nation's growth goals. Recent developments in this latter respect cannot be judged propitious in many of the world's regions.

While the intellectual content of the economic development process remains a matter of some controversy today, the actual record of growth in various parts of the world in the years to the early 1970s did lend support to the decisive role of *quality* inputs in growth achievement in rich lands. And the relative *unimportance* of the returns to quality inputs in poor lands was held most responsible for their uncertain economic performance. The accompanying diagram (Figure 2-1) reflects these contrasts impressionistically.[7] It suggests that the growth returns to effective leadership-for-growth became progressively more important in total growth of rich lands, as against the growth returns from more labor and more capital of constant quality. On the poor nation side, limited performance from quality inputs resulted in much lower rates of growth than supplies of capital resources and of numbers of workers could have permitted.

The course of development in both rich-land and poor-land components of the world was interrupted by the world recession of the mid-1970s. In some measure, this setback was itself a reflection of a leadership crisis. But even if more emphasis is given to the role of the natural resource crises of the 1970s—to food, raw materials, petroleum—recovery has been hampered by quality input difficulties stemming from diffusion of quality inputs in rich lands and from diversion of interest from quality to quantity inputs in poor lands. Both prompt conservative expectations of long-term rates of economic growth, in rich as well as poor nations, (Chapter III).

Intensity-of-use data were assembled for essentially the same time intervals, 1951-1975, with occasional data for 1934-1938. They are of course presented here on the same regional bases as were GDP, population and GDP/population. Again, materials use data are from the accepted world sources, notably national

---

[6]In particular, *Population by Sex and Age for Regions and Countries, 1950-2000, As Assessed in 1973: Medium Variant*, ESA/P/WP60, 25 February 1976.

[7]For a brief summary account of the underlying economic arguments, with references to the theoretical literature and an illustration in the case of India, see Wilfred Malenbaum, *Modern India's Economy*, Merrill, 1971, pp. 117-23.

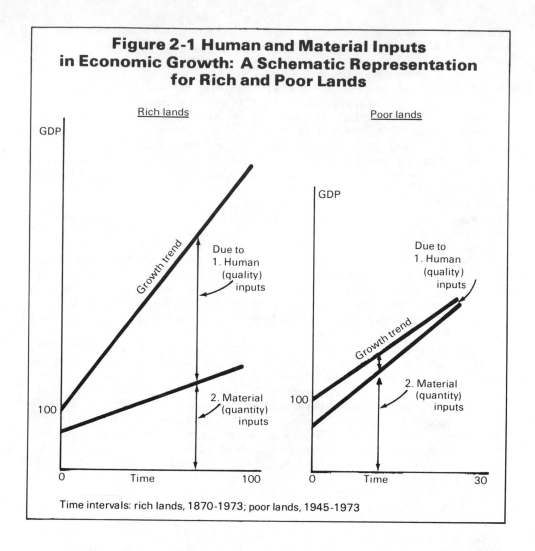

Figure 2-1 Human and Material Inputs in Economic Growth: A Schematic Representation for Rich and Poor Lands

Rich lands

Poor lands

GDP

GDP

Growth trend

Due to
1. Human
(quality)
inputs

Due to
1. Human
(quality)
inputs

Growth trend

100

100

2. Material
(quantity)
inputs

2. Material
(quantity)
inputs

0   Time   100

0   Time   30

Time intervals: rich lands, 1870-1973; poor lands, 1945-1973

and international organizations in the public sector, e.g., U.S. Bureau of Mines, U.K. Statistical Summary of the Mineral Industry, U.N. Department of Economic and Social Affairs, and occasional specialized private groups associated with producing and processing interests (e.g., Germany's *Metal Statistics*). Specific sources appear in the Appendix Tables and the Bibliography. Insofar as possible "use" was considered on the basis of raw materials as such, i.e., ore, metal. The consumption concept was "apparent consumption," defined as production of raw material minus exports plus imports plus change in stocks. Foreign trade and inventory adjustment did not take account of raw materials embodied in *final finished* products. Again, the data are broadly available, with exceptions already noted and appropriately referenced in this Report. However available are published statistics in some form, much materials consumption data have not previously been assembled in consistent sets of regional tables on a world basis.

The intensity-of-use measure was of course obtained by dividing apparent consumption by the GDP figures discussed above. It is this measure that receives major research attention in this study. As already indicated, the very concept has a technological ring. It is apparent that the values of these measures differ significantly as among the world's regions, as they do in each region over time. Presumably, the measure for each i depends upon industrialization, economic sophistication, resources endowment and other factors for which the world does offer a wide range of patterns. And these factors change over time, notably with industrial and economic development. Use of materials inputs must be associated with the specific products and services a nation produces— the output of automobiles, or the miles people travel in a year, or the extent of electrification, as examples. And every measure of materials use should be accounted for fully in such itemized outputs. To do this would certainly be a major research undertaking even for the relatively few countries where statistics on use detail are available. Any projected use-intensity would require many specific assumptions about future product use. Hence, reliance needs to be put on more general attributes of the demand for materials, derived from past relationships and from the theory that helps explain past use of materials.

Trends and patterns of past intensity-of-use data were studied; they offer several possibilities for the future. On occasion, the past record suggested a more or less direct extrapolation to 1985 or to 2000. More common was evidence of a reversing pattern with intensities growing over a period and then contracting. There is evidence of some association with per capita income levels. On the whole, intensity-of-use measures for all regions of the world do seem to reveal some systematic patterns. These are discussed below, with special regard to the following factors: actual changes in final goods and services (in which the materials are inputs) as per capita income grows; the development of new technologies that make for more efficient materials use; the possibilities of substitution among materials (or with other intermediate goods such as synthetics) as technology, demand and supply alter relative materials prices. All these and the extensive analytic and descriptive literature on materials use do provide some guides for projecting the appropriate intensity level for 1985 and 2000 (see Figure 2-2). As in the case of GDP, economic theory helped also, particularly theoretical doctrine on commodity substitution with demand and technological change, and with the price and policy adjustments related to these changes.

In the last analysis, however, systematic consideration of these guides and possibilities needed to be supplemented by the judgment of the research worker. In this present NSF-sponsored report as in the initial NCMP study, this subjective input was the responsibility of one individual, the principal researcher on this project. As with the "answers" for rates of national growth to the years 1985 and 2000, the "answers" on intensity-of-use of each material in those years reflected consistent judgments, conditioned by a vast assembly of pertinent data (and by published and other expert opinion), the economic rationale of past performance, and theories of economic equilibrium, change, and growth.

Materials requirements for 1985 and 2000, with comparable statistics on historical use, are treated in Chapter V. The "answers" for the future permit ready comparisons of materials consumption over time and among important subdivisions of the world. They also provide a point of brief departure to questions of supply-demand relationships and to materials-supply and economic growth relationships.

Finally, emphasis must again be given to the truth that the main components of the research program rest on a common basic assumption: the growth of nations has an *internal dynamic*. That is, long-term growth is not governed by supply limitations of any specific input materials nor is it limited by any inelasticity of total output imposed by supply or demand of materials. This assump-

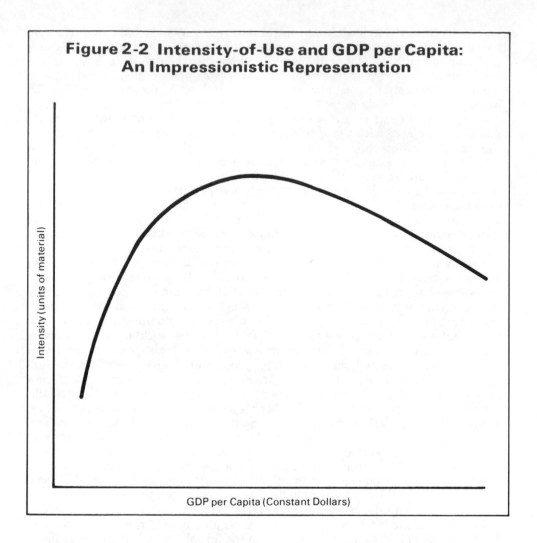

Figure 2-2 Intensity-of-Use and GDP per Capita:
An Impressionistic Representation

Intensity (units of material)

GDP per Capita (Constant Dollars)

tion made it possible to project national and world economic growth in one part of the research effort without regard to the materials needs appraised in the other part of the study. A nation meets its needs for materials in the pursuit of its economic, social, and political objectives. This assumption is consistent with the theory of economic growth held to be relevant to experience in the modern world of the past two centuries or so. In addition, the research on past materials consumption, and indeed the results developed below, are themselves testimony to the diversity of materials usage in the modern world. As relative supplies shift, as demands alter, as techniques of use change, as price ratios vary, rules of operation are altered. These adjustments are the tools by which man and society obtain and use materials they need. This is how it has been; the extensive past experience augurs well for the future.

But the tools must cope with what promise to be progressively greater tasks. Poor nations must have higher levels of living; populations grow at record rates; minerals production generates environmental hazards. There is need for continuous and imaginative study of the alternatives in supply and requirements of materials, and for governmental and intergovernmental policy and action based on such study. Still, the past record tells us that such efforts can be undertaken with the expectation that the world's materials resources can continue to serve the world's aspirations for social and economic progress. The world's materials resources will govern such objectives only if research and policy needs are neglected.

Chapter III
World Economic Growth:
The Prospect for 1985 and 2000

The record of national growth throughout the world over the past thirty years or so has been subjected to extensive analysis. Scientific mastery of the determinants of national growth was thought to have been achieved: fiscal and monetary policies, resource and knowledge transfers became commonplace tools, broadly available to nations through a growing body of practitioners in business, public and academic life. This intellectual achievement was indeed paralleled by an extraordinary growth achievement for almost twenty-five years from mid-century. GDP grew at very rapid rates, seemingly without past parallel, and quite generally throughout the regions of the world. Despite record levels of population growth, output per person moved ahead even in the poor lands, and again without early parallels.

But the miracle faltered. Neither theoretical knowledge nor recent achievement offers today any assured growth prospects for the decades ahead. Despite the impressive overall growth performance in third world lands, careful analytic studies have for some years been suggesting that so-called "quality" inputs have played a progressively diminished role in national growth. Indeed, poor-nation economies and societies were becoming more dualistic, with widening gaps between labor-intensive and capital-intensive sectors, between an increasing percentage of poor and a small percentage of rich. With such internal developments, these nations were not able to make effective use of their actual productive endowments, nor of the further increments in these resources potentially available to them. Basically national leaders in these lands were not able or not willing to stimulate, in the public or the private sector, greater output per person on the part of the maximum possible segment of their populations.

Note has been made of the contrast in growth forces in the rich and successful lands and in those in the faltering economies of the poor lands, even in the years from 1950 through 1973. But by the mid-1970s the contrast has become less apparent. The rich economies were themselves suffering from internal divisiveness, from leadership activities geared to gains of only part of the society. In any event, the present world recession emerges as an economic state not responsive to the growth tools of past decades. In rich as well as poor nations, new tasks await new leadership. New quality inputs that will serve to integrate each national economy are essential if high growth rates are again to be achieved. Supplies of labor, technology and related skills—standard inputs of theories of growth—continue of course to be needed. But historical analyses of actual growth in rich lands on the one side, and of world experience with accelerated development efforts in poor nations over two-three decades on the other, suggest that supplies of the traditional inputs in whatever measure cannot of themselves assure sustained economic progress.

Man and society seem less able to use these standard inputs effectively. This has become apparent in recent decades even as supplies (including education, technology and skills) have expanded dramatically in most of the world's countries. The poor nations need to engender deeper commitments to economic expansion on the part of workers, so many of whom are essentially self-employed and hence decision-makers. It is necessary that national institutions involve these workers more directly in development activity. The early priorities for government policy need to focus on increments in employment, with emphasis on the *compatibility* of maximum employment *and* maximum output goals in what can be characterized as an essentially persistent state of disequilibrium in the economy. These requirements were emphasized with respect to problems of poor-nation growth in *NCMP 1973,* but the current economic outlook for the world's rich lands calls for a similar emphasis. Underutilized people and underutilized capital facilities and underutilized technological knowledge and skills defy efficient generation of GDP; institutional changes and new operational methods need exploration, testing and implementation. The quality of leadership over the next decades will be a fundamental determinant of the level of economic progress achieved.

Unhappily, the operational course to that end is not straightforward. The gross product outlook for 1985 and 2000 cannot be any mechanical extrapolation of the record of the past twenty-five years or so. The rates of future growth offered here for the next decade and for the turn of the century reflect judgments on the extent to which new and different economic and social policies will in fact emerge in the various regions of the world. Similar considerations prevailed in *NCMP 1973,* but developments over the intervening years prompt a greater respect for the difficulties to be overcome.

The actual growth rates to 2000 used in the present report differ for the most part from those applied in *NCMP 1973.* On the whole, the persistent development problems in the rich lands over the past five years have altered in some degree the earlier growth expectations for the rich relative to the poor categories of nations. It is true that implementation of programs for quality inputs has long-term roots in the developed lands. But the need to shift to an employment emphasis poses difficult decisions in their capital-intensive economic structures. Nor can progress in the poor nations be dramatic, however great the development potential such activities can promise. And poor-nation preoccupation with old formulas on economic development may at best offer occasional short-term gains and limited long-term growth benefits. So, pending pursuit of new development strategies, GDP average growth rates are expected to have low levels relative to those of the 1951-75 era.

Finally, the projected growth rates reflect the judgment of the principal investigator, after full consideration of other research appraisals currently available on the prospects for world economic development.

Tables 3-1.1—3-1.3 give the annual rates of growth estimated from 1975 to 1985 and to 2000 for GDP, population and GDP per person, respectively.

Some historical base data are included in these tables for ready comparison; further detail for past years is available in Appendix Tables III-1—III-3. Corresponding data for actual average levels of GDP, population and GDP per person (U.S. $s, 1971 prices) are given in text Tables 3-2.1—3-2.3. (Again, Appendix Tables III-1—III-3 are more complete for the data of past years.) All these magnitudes are reported for the world, its two major subdivisions and separately for ten world regions. Where *NCMP 1973* provided comparable estimates for the year 2000, these are shown alongside the projections to that date in the present study.

Table 3-1.1
World GDP: 1951-2000 Annual Growth Rates*

Region	1951-75	1975-85	1975-2000**	
1. W. Europe	4.5	3.3	3.2	(3.5)
2. Japan	9.3	4.2	4.1	(5.0)
3. ODL	4.7	3.4	3.3	(3.75)
4. U.S.S.R.	5.5	3.6	3.4	(4.0)
5. E. Europe	4.9	3.7	3.5	(3.5)
6. Africa	5.1	3.5	3.4	(3.4)
7. Asia	4.9	3.3	3.2	(3.5)
8. L. America	5.6	3.7	3.6	(3.75)
9. China	4.3	3.5	3.3	(4.2)
10. U.S.	3.6	3.3	3.2	(3.8)
Totals				
11. World	4.7	3.5	3.3	(3.8)
12. Non-U.S. World	5.2	3.5	3.4	(3.8)
13. Poor Nations	5.0	3.5	3.4	(3.8)
14. Rich Nations	4.6	3.5	3.3	(3.9)

Source: Table 3-2.1; also see text, Chapter III.

* Annual rates based on 5-year periods; thus 1951-75 refers to 20-year period from 1951-55 to 1971-75.

1975-85 refers to 12.5-year period from 1971-75 to a 5-year period centered at 1985.

1975-2000 refers to 27.5-year period from 1971-75 to a 5-year period centered at 2000.

** Bracketed rates are comparable magnitudes estimated in an earlier study, *NCMP 1973* (see text).

Table 3-1.2
World Population: 1951-2000 Annual Growth Rates*

Region	1951-75	1975-85	1975-2000**	
1. W. Europe	0.9	0.8	1.0	(1.1)
2. Japan	1.1	0.9	0.8	(1.0)
3. ODL	2.3	2.0	1.8	(1.3)
4. U.S.S.R.	1.4	1.0	1.1	(1.5)
5. E. Europe	0.8	0.8	1.0	(1.0)
6. Africa	2.4	2.7	2.4	(2.6)
7. Asia	2.5	2.7	2.4	(2.2)
8. L. America	2.9	2.8	2.6	(2.8)
9. China	1.8	1.6	1.4	(1.4)
10. U.S.	1.5	1.0	1.0	(1.2)
Totals				
11. World	2.0	· 2.0	1.8	(1.8)
12. Non-U.S. World	2.0	2.0	1.9	(1.9)
13. Poor Nations	2.3	2.4	2.1	(1.9)
14. Rich Nations	1.2	1.0	1.0	(1.2)

Source: Table 3-2.2; also see text, Chapter III.   *As in Table 3-1.1.   **As in Table 3-1.1.

Table 3-1.3
World GDP Per Capita: 1951-2000 Annual Growth Rates*

Region	1951-75	1975-85	1975-2000**	
1. W. Europe	3.6	2.5	2.2	(2.5)
2. Japan	8.2	3.3	3.3	(4.0)
3. ODL	2.4	1.4	1.5	(2.5)
4. U.S.S.R.	4.1	2.6	2.3	(2.6)
5. E. Europe	4.1	2.9	2.5	(2.5)
6. Africa	2.7	0.8	1.0	(0.9)
7. Asia	2.4	0.6	0.8	(1.3)
8. L. America	2.7	0.9	1.0	(1.0)
9. China	2.5	1.9	1.9	(2.9)
10. U.S.	2.1	2.3	2.2	(2.6)
Totals				
11. World	2.7	1.5	1.5	(2.0)
12. Non-U.S. World	3.2	1.5	1.5	(2.0)
13. Poor Nations	2.7	1.1	1.3	(1.9)
14. Rich Nations	3.4	2.5	2.3	(2.7)

Source: Table 3-2.3; also see text, Chapter III.

*As in Table 3-1.1.

**As in Table 3-1.1.

Table 3-2.1
World GDP: 1951-2000
(Billions of U.S. $, 1971 prices)

Region	1951-55	1971-75	1985	2000**	
1. W. Europe	389	936	1405	2226	(2590)
2. Japan	44	258	431	779	(1070)
3. ODL	73	183	278	447	(490)
4. U.S.S.R.	210	617	960	1547	(1680)
5. E. Europe	86	227	357	585	(575)
6. Africa	26	71	109	178	(185)
7. Asia	77	201	302	478	(680)
8. L. America	67	200	315	529	(620)
9. China	62	144	221	352	(480)
10. U.S.	557	1122	1684	2668	(3135)
Totals					
11. World	1591	3960	6062	9789	(11495)
12. Non-U.S. World	1034	2838	4378	7121	(8360)
13. Poor Nations	232	617	947	1537	(1965)
14. Rich Nations	1359	3344	5115	8252	(9530)

Source: See Appendix Table III-1, also see text, Chapter III.   **As in Table 3-1.1.

Table 3-2.2
World Population: 1951-2000
(Millions of People)

Region	1951-55	1971-75	1985	2000**	
1. W. Europe	314	379	419	498	(510)
2. Japan	87	108	122	133	(140)
3. ODL	41	64	82	105	(90)
4. U.S.S.R.	189	250	282	336	(375)
5. E. Europe	110	130	144	171	(170)
6. Africa	218	354	493	680	(700)
7. Asia	726	1199	1672	2301	(2160)
8. L. America	170	299	422	605	(650)
9. China	594	852	1038	1248	(1335)
10. U.S.	160	214	242	281	(300)
Totals					
11. World	2609	3848	4916	6358	(6430)
12. Non-U.S. World	2448	3635	4674	6077	(6130)
13. Poor Nations	1708	2703	3625	4834	(4845)
14. Rich Nations	901	1144	1291	1524	(1585)

Source: See Appendix Table III-2, also see text, Chapter III.   **As in Table 3-1.1.

Table 3-2.3
World GDP Per Capita: 1951-2000
(U.S. $, 1971 prices)

Region	1951-55	1971-75	1985	2000**	
1. W. Europe	1238	2469	3353	4470	(5059)
2. Japan	507	2389	3532	5857	(7643)
3. ODL	1788	2869	3390	4257	(5444)
4. U.S.S.R.	1106	2469	3404	4604	(4480)
5. E. Europe	788	1747	2479	3421	(3382)
6. Africa	120	202	221	262	(264)
7. Asia	106	168	181	208	(315)
8. L. America	393	671	746	874	(954)
9. China	104	168	213	282	(360)
10. U.S.	3472	5250	6959	9495	(10450)
Totals					
11. World	609	1029	1233	1540	(1788)
12. Non-U.S. World	422	781	937	1172	(1364)
13. Poor Nations	136	228	261	318	(406)
14. Rich Nations	1508	2922	3962	5415	(6013)

Source: See Appendix Table III-3; also see text, Chapter III.   **As in Table 3-1.1

World GDP is shown to be growing at an average rate of 3.5 percent between 1971-75 and 1985, and by 3.3 percent between 1971-75 and 2000. These contrast with an actual growth rate of 4.7 percent per year, 1951-75. Total real product will thus increase by more than 50 percent from 1971-75 to 1985 and by 150 percent from 1971-75 to 2000. GDP estimates for 2000 in the world as a whole, and indeed in the U.S.-non-U.S. and in the poor nation-rich nation subgroups of the world, are lower than were the GDP projections for 2000 in *NCMP 1973*. If the 1951-75 growth rates were expected to continue, world GDP in 2000 would be shown in the $13-14 trillion range, in contrast to an $11.5 trillion figure in *NCMP 1973* and just below $10 trillion in the present Report (Table 3-2.1). Such lower levels are now considered appropriate broadly over the entire world. In some small degree they do reflect the later data (1973 through 1977) available for the present Report: the actual scale of world recession exceeded pre-1973 expectations. But as indicated earlier the basic reasons for the present projections of significantly lower GDP growth rates stem from the current state of economic growth theory and knowledge. While *NCMP 1973* was alert and explicit with regard to new forces in the economic growth process, their nature and strength have taken clearer form over the last five years or so. It seems hard to believe today that only a few years back (during 1965-73, as noted earlier) many demand projections for raw materials were based on average GDP growth rates in the 5-6 percent range for a thirty-year time interval. This would have meant a doubling of world GDP each 12-13 years—a five-fold increase. The world estimates of Table 3-1.1 foresee a doubling interval of at least twenty years with an increase below 2.5-fold.

A few additional observations on Tables 3-2.1—3-2.3 may be helpful. Thus U.S. GDP continues its decline as a share of world GDP, but the rate of decline is significantly smaller in 1975-2000 than it was during 1951-75. As Table 3-1.1 shows, these postwar decades were marked by appreciably higher GDP growth rates in the non-U.S. world. Special circumstances were contributory here: reconstruction activities in Europe and Japan, the overall conservatism of domestic economic policy in the U.S. In the future, the challenges outlined earlier will confront economic growth efforts in all areas, as is also revealed in Table 3-1.1. The poor nations together have made slow but persistent progress as reflected in their share of world GDP. In 1985 and 2000, their share will increase above current levels of some 15 percent, but only by a percentage point or so.

Despite the present outlook for lower GDP growth rates, Tables 3-1.3 and 3-2.3 show continued progress in levels of GDP per person for all the world's regions in 1985 and 2000. The average GDP per person level in the world's poor nations will continue to *decline* as ratios of the average level in the world's rich lands. The data of Table 3-2.3 and of Appendix Tables III-1—III-3 reveal a significantly better relative growth performance for Mainland China than for the other poor nations together. As already suggested, this is attributed in important measure to Chinese growth efforts that serve to enhance labor productivity for very large parts of China's population. No comparable experience has emerged for very large population groups in other poor regions. Given the major differences in population growth rates in the poor nations and in the rich nations—past and future in Table 3-1.2—to narrow the gap in per capita product will require significantly higher GDP growth rates in the former category of nations. This cannot be considered a probable development over the next decade or generation.

Note is made here of the contrast between this last statement and the seemingly much more hopeful possibilities recently publicized by the United Nations on the basis of a new study of the world growth outlook.[8] Essentially, this publication presents a prospect for the achievement by 2000 of a very much more rapid rate of GDP growth in all the poor lands taken together. It speaks of annual growth rates for these nations in the 5.5-7.5 percent range, with an overall average (1970-2000) of 6.9 percent or more. This contrasts with the actual 5 percent of 1951-75 and the 3.4 percent projected for 1975-2000 in Table 3-1.1. The U.N. study also speaks of some slackening in the growth rates of rich nations, to an average of 3.6 percent (as against the 3.3 percent of Table 3-1.1). *Mostly* the poor-nation acceleration would result from changes in existing political, social and institutional deterrents to economic expansion in these lands, although in some measure it would also benefit from significant increments in new capital inflows somehow sparked by poor-nation endowments in raw materials. The deceleration in the rich nation growth rate is presented in the U.N. study as the obverse effect of a net transfer of resources to the poor nations.

There are important gains to the world in a restructured world GDP which generates income flows that are more egalitarian among nations than are current and recent flows. Social and psychological gains might well exceed whatever economic losses could occur. Indeed there are strong arguments that such *noneconomic* benefits might actually be accompanied by *economic* gains, that maximum economic gains do require some such restructured flow of world GDP. Of greater concern than the *desirability* is the *possibility* of generating significantly changed international income flows over the next decades. The social, political and institutional adjustments needed to this end are essentially unspecified in the U.N. study; there is broad reference to domestic property and income redistribution objectives within the poor nations. The achievement of such goals would require a very new and very different approach to the bulk of the population on the part of indigenous leadership and power groups.

Current development emphasis in most of the poor nations draws from the activities of what was called the "Committee of 77" in the U.N., with its focus on the potential economic and political gains from the natural resource endowments of the poor lands. This emphasis actually plays down the fundamental role of *internal* political, social, institutional and economic impediments to progress. Without a new philosophy on broad participation in action programs *within* the poor lands, the scope for additional growth gains through capital transfers continues to remain limited. On the other side, it is hard to foresee international transfers over the next decade which are appreciably larger in relative magnitude than have recently prevailed. Nor is this outlook attributable to donor nation concern that larger transfers would reduce the rich world's own rates of GDP growth. For they need not; the fundamental determinants of economic expansion today lie outside any essentially mechanical and material endowment area.

It is for such reasons that the present study has made use of GDP developments summarized in the sets of Tables 3-1 and 3-2. These are held to portray realistic orders of magnitude for world economic expansion over the next two to three decades. Given these estimates for 1985 and 2000, both the GDP and the GDP per capita elements of the materials demand relationships are in hand. Intensity-of-materials-use, the third element, is discussed in the next Chapter of this Report.

---

[8]*The Future of the World Economy*, A United Nations Study by Wassily Leontief, *et al.*, New York, Oxford University Press, 1977.

Chapter IV
Intensity-of-Use

The preceding argument has drawn upon relevant theory and observation to establish orders of magnitude for future rates of growth in total product, in population and thus in future GDP per person. These estimates were directed at time spans pertinent to current action for economic and social change: 5-10 years, by 1985 and a generation, by 2000. Estimates for these dates were made separately for each of the ten component parts in which the world is considered here. For reasons explicit in the argument, these future growth rates for total product and per capita product are different, and lower, than were those presented in the 1973 study. Indeed, the present conclusion is that output growth rates over the next two to three decades will average significantly below those prevailing in the decades from 1950-1975. However, the basic thrust of the 1973 argument remains the same: human, quality aspects of the world's societies provide the propelling forces for economic expansion. Judgments on these inputs, not on any quantity of materials inputs, were the decisive elements in this study's determination of the product figures for 1985 and 2000.

Nonetheless, per capita product is expected to be growing throughout the world over the period to 2000. The average per capita income gap between the rich and poor nations continues to widen absolutely and relatively. And the world continues to aspire to economic progress.

Important quantitative differences are also revealed in the new study with respect to the future levels of the third element basic to the methodology of the present analysis: the intensity-of-use of raw materials. As indicated in the Introduction, the present work included a larger number of materials and a lengthier time span than did the initial study. These provided an improved base for factual observation. The historical results, average intensity-of-use by five-year periods for each of the twelve raw materials in each regional grouping, are given in Appendix Tables IV-1 to IV-12. The patterns revealed in these data provided support for projections of generally lower I-U levels than were indicated by the information available for the 1973 report.

Again the basic data strongly endorse the earlier argument about the changing "constants" of the relationship between materials use and total output of goods and services. The enlarged body of data also supports the early hypothesis of systematic relationships between intensity-of-use levels in a region and its real per capita product over time. The changing intensity patterns emerge clearly in text Tables 4-1 to 4-12; so also do the I-U, GDP per capita relationships in Figures 4-1 to 4-12. These tables are first discussed in general terms in the following pages. Specific consideration of individual materials then provides further detail on past data as well as the basis for specific I-U projections. All the considerations underlying this presentation on the I-U variable parallel those provided in the 1973 report.[9] As there, the critical factors lie in the evolving GDP structure of the individual world regions and in the materials substitution/displacement through market and national policy forces, especially under the stimulus of technological developments.

The text tables make clear that for all materials considered here—other than aluminum (9) and with qualification the platinum group of metals (10)—world intensity of use has already reached historical peak levels, and mostly a decade or more back. By 1970, these levels were below what had been assumed for that year in *NCMP 1973*. Moreover, the data through 1973 do document declines that had not yet become apparent in the earlier work. It is in these respects that the present study provides strong additional empirical strength to the hypotheses on I-U patterns presented in *NCMP 1973*.

This inverted-U pattern for the world tends to be revealed even more clearly in the subtotals for I-U in the non-U.S. world and in the rich nations alone. This follows because there actually are two other reasonably distinct I-U patterns in the 1951-1975 data for the U.S. alone and for the poor nations alone. In the former, the turning point in I-U was reached at an early date, and for important raw materials (including iron, steel, copper, zinc, tin, among other metals) prior to 1951. The present data seem simply to show persistent I-U declines in the U.S. On the part of the poor nations there is usually the reverse pattern of fairly steady increases in I-U over the period of record here. This last was also inferred from the less complete record in the earlier study. Now however there is some evidence of slackening in the growth of I-U in some materials in important developing lands among the poor nations. In contrast to the earlier view in *NCMP 1973*, the present prospect is that I-U for most materials will *not* continue to expand in poor nations until high levels of economic development are in fact achieved. Rather, the effects of technological advance elsewhere are spread to them at a relatively early stage of economic growth. An upward I-U thrust from the poor nations was earlier considered to be some counter on a world basis to a downward I-U thrust from the rich nations. The present study provides a somewhat modified general position; the overall force to lower intensity-of-use for raw materials is a stronger one than was suggested in the early work.

In sum, there is for most materials a broad world picture of declining use intensity. A critical component is the position of the U.S., usually the world's primary consumer of materials and from early years the world's predominant industrialized nation. In the U.S. there has long been a persistent downward movement in I-U. Other rich lands reflect the same pattern, with turning points for I-U levels at later dates than in the U.S., perhaps as they reached some specific level of industrial/economic progress. (A turning point with per capita GDP level of some 2000 U.S. 1971 dollars was suggested in *NCMP 1973*.) The tendency to lower I-U levels was also explained for rich lands in terms of the contribution to that end made by technological progress. The general evidence now is that this factor may begin to be manifest at relatively low-income stages of development through the spread of technology from the rich nations. In any event, several important low-income nations demonstrate flattening, if not

---

[9]*NCMP 1973*, pp. 9-10 especially.

declining, I-U levels even in the 1970s—and even before the spread of any influence from the current world recession. Finally of course it is possible that the force of structural change and substitution/displacement through technological progress can *expand* materials use per unit of GDP. Among the materials studied here, the sole evidence of long-period net increases in I-U *is* in aluminum and to much lesser degree in platinum-group metals. Currently these forces seem also to contribute a slackening, if not yet a declining element in aluminum I-U.

There is another range of general considerations that might be noted here: the differences in level of I-U for a given material as among rich countries particularly at a given point of time and/or at a given level of real GDP per person. These are readily observed along the time columns of Tables 4-1 to 4-12, as along the GDP per capita axes of Figures 4-1 to 4-12. For many commodities it is the I-U level in Japan that is most striking, although there are occasional high ranges for the U.S.S.R. and at times Eastern Europe. Such distinct differences in general I-U levels need much more study than could be undertaken for the present Report. But a few general observations are appropriate. For Japan (and this would probably be true for West Germany as for some Eastern European countries) the sheer magnitude of the postwar industrialization drive in the national effort has yielded I-U levels that exceed what was the historical record in most developed lands. Also relevant is the relative share of industrial exports in GDP. As noted above the "apparent consumption" concept used in the present study does not adjust for the foreign trade of raw materials incorporated as inputs of processed goods exported and utilized abroad. For Japan this net outflow from "apparent consumption" has been appreciably above the levels in Europe and North America, for example. The same phenomenon, albeit in more moderate form, may be concealed in the data for some materials in individual countries included in a region composed of a number of separate lands. Similarly, the higher levels of I-U (at comparable GDP per capita) for iron and steel in the U.S.S.R. testify to the very high ratio of heavy industry in an already very high capital formation ratio in the Russian economy during the postwar years. At that time the U.S.S.R. gross capital formation percentage was running at about twice the level of the comparable U.S. percentage. High I-U also reflects the relatively larger U.S.S.R. emphasis on military goods production in those decades. The somewhat lower intensities for copper, zinc and other nonferrous metals in Russia may mirror the offsetting role of consumer goods in total product of the U.S.S.R. over the period 1951-1975.

Finally, these general patterns of the text Tables 4 are supported by the additional time-interval data of the Appendix Tables, IV-1—IV-12. On the whole, the data of the present study endorse strongly the regularity of behavior of the I-U variable for materials throughout the world, as hypothesized and reported in *NCMP 1973*.

Crude Steel (1), Iron Ore (2)

National consumption of iron and steel is influenced by a country's level of national income, the standard of living of its people and the structure of its economy. The changing levels and composition of demand for the total of final goods and services thus exercise a dominant force upon the level and pattern of intensities of use of these materials. It is not surprising therefore that the data of Tables 4-1 and 4-2 and the scatter-arrays of Figures 4-1 and 4-2 conform closely with the general observations above, which were based on relationships that emerged from the range of raw materials studied. The influence of demand for the total of final goods and services has been a dominant force on the iron and steel intensities. The world's developed nations had in early years expanded their use of iron ore and of steel more rapidly than GDP as modern transportation, industry and construction increased their composite share of GDP. I-U then declined rapidly; service activities moved steadily ahead with expanding per capita product. More "services" did of course involve heavy-goods outlays, as in the rapid growth of such major infrastructures as highways. But on the whole higher GDP per person brought a shift in demand to less steel-intensive variants even of such final goods as buildings and automobiles. Among the rich countries the historical record of steel I-U raises questions only with respect to the data for Eastern Europe, where early peak I-U levels are found in rather low per capita product ranges. Here the demand explanation probably also pertains: there were large heavy equipment exports to the U.S.S.R. in the first postwar decade. Also, there is some evidence of early inefficiencies in steel production in that area; use of open-hearth furnaces persisted long after these were replaced elsewhere by less wasteful steel manufacturing processes.

In the world's less developed nations these intensities reflect the expanding phases of GDP growth. Most of these nations are increasingly involved in infrastructural projects—railroads and other transportation and communications systems, dams for irrigation and power, electric utilities and comparable steel-intensive works. In addition, the process of economic diversification and industrialization brought shifts of investment to heavy industry at the relative cost of capital expansion in consumer goods industry. All this contributes to national output that is more steel and iron ore intensive. Moreover total national income in these nations did move ahead rapidly over the decades from 1950. Thus rate of GDP growth and GDP diversification served to stimulate use of iron and steel. While the intensity Tables (4-1 and 4-2 of the text and IV-1 and IV-2 of the Appendix) suggest uneven expansion, 1971-75 yields peak levels for the period since 1951; I-U reflects the strength of the forces of demand.

Technological change and substitution of materials also played an important role in affecting I-U of iron and steel, and particularly in the rich nations. From the early 1950's there has been continuous technical innovation in the various stages of the steel production process, including the increased importance of agglomeration and beneficiation of iron ore, the replacement of open-hearth furnaces with more efficient basic oxygen systems and electric-arc furnaces, and the introduction of continuous casting. These developments have permitted greater general economy in iron ore use (due to better product yields per ton of raw material) and have prevented much steel waste in the final processing stages. Economy of material use was also enhanced by technical progress yielding final products that are more frugal steel users, as in advances in miniaturization, increased standardization and all-around design improvements. Finally, increased substitution for steel in many uses by such materials as reinforced concrete, aluminum and plastics, and by other alloys also contributes to falls in intensity. These innovations have been strong forces for I-U declines in rich lands, supplementing the I-U effects attributed to the changing level and composition of GDP in these regions. The technological and substitution factors are expected to continue and even intensify. They support the demand forces to assure the persistent I-U declines to 1985 and 2000.

Technological and substitution forces are of course also manifest in the poor nations and they have served to mitigate the upward trends caused by GDP growth and structural change. While open-hearth processes have become far less important throughout the world, and while available iron resources and hydroelectric power encourage use of electric arc furnaces and direct-reduction processes in some poor nations, the prospect of parallel applications of new methods remains small over the next decade and generation. Alternative products are less competitive, steel scrap is less available and iron ore is often

Table 4-1
Intensity-of-Use: Crude Steel, 1951-2000
(1000 metric tons per billion $ GDP, 1971 prices)

Region	1951-55	1961-65	1971-75	1985	2000
1. W. Europe	127.4	188.9	155.8	135	120
2. Japan	142.2	345.2	274.6	260	230
3. ODL	128.4	150.7	149.1	135	120
4. U.S.S.R.	163.2	202.8	208.9	190	170
5. E. Europe	265.8	235.8	202.4	190	170
6. Africa	49.3	57.6	68.9	75	85
7. Asia	45.7	101.9	145.6	150	150
8. L. America	76.2	122.6	124.8	130	135
9. China	36.0	144.8	201.5	200	190
10. U.S.	163.5	136.9	120.6	100	80
Totals					
11. World	141.8	171.1	162.2	148	133
12. Non-U.S. World	130.1	186.7	178.6	166	153
13. Poor Nations	52.3	113.0	142.8	147	147
14. Rich Nations	157.1	181.0	165.7	148	130

Source: Appendix Table IV-1; also see text Chapter IV.

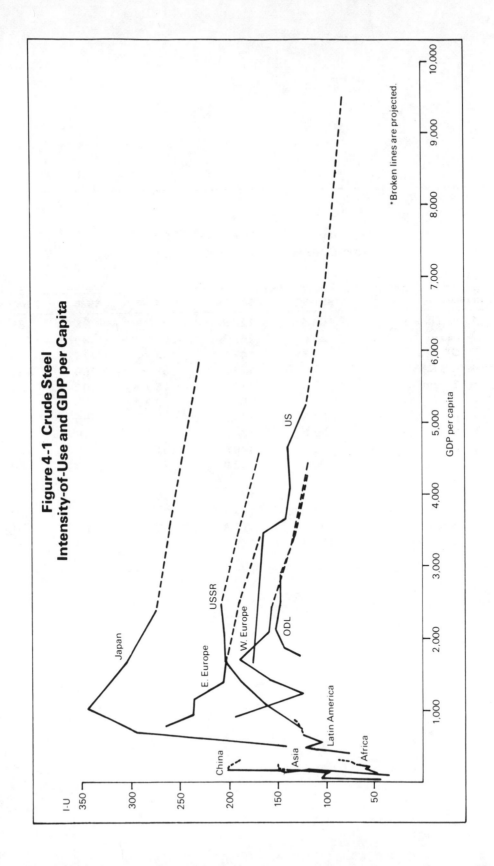

**Figure 4-1 Crude Steel
Intensity-of-Use and GDP per Capita**

I-U

350

300

250

200

150

100

50

Japan

E. Europe

USSR

W. Europe

US

ODL

China

Asia

Latin America

Africa

1,000

2,000

3,000

4,000

5,000

6,000

7,000

8,000

9,000

10,000

GDP per capita

*Broken lines are projected.

35

Table 4-2
Intensity-of-Use: Iron Ore, 1951-2000
(1000 metric tons per billion $ GDP, 1971 prices)

Region	1951-55	1961-65	1971-75	1985	2000
1. W. Europe	104.4	126.9	101.0	95	85
2. Japan	67.0	267.3	204.5	180	165
3. ODL	81.7	142.3	132.9	125	110
4. U.S.S.R.	137.1	172.5	157.1	150	135
5. E. Europe	71.9	117.7	115.7	100	85
6. Africa	46.4	57.9	53.2	70	80
7. Asia	27.9	46.2	49.8	60	70
8. L. America	22.8	67.8	73.5	80	90
9. China	35.4	140.5	161.1	175	185
10. U.S.	106.9	92.9	76.1	63	50
Totals					
11. World	95.0	121.8	109.1	103	94
12. Non-U.S. World	88.5	134.9	122.1	118	110
13. Poor Nations	30.5	75.8	83.4	95	104
14. Rich Nations	106.0	129.6	113.7	104	92

Source: Appendix Table IV-2; also see text, Chapter IV.

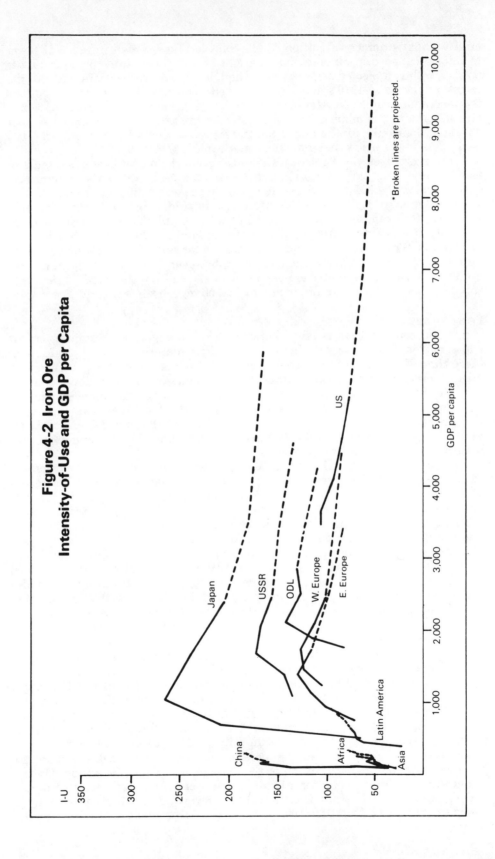

Figure 4-2 Iron Ore
Intensity-of-Use and GDP per Capita

* Broken lines are projected.

37

used without prior beneficiation. Such considerations weigh in favor of lower technological horizons in many poor nations over the years to 1985 and 2000. I-U levels are thus projected at persistently high levels over these years. Indeed, the record of the early 1970's actually prompted higher steel intensity projections than were foreseen in *NCMP 1973* for 2000. In this regard, the steel situation is unusual among the materials studied here. At any rate this pertains to the poor nation outlook only; for the rich lands and for the world and non-U.S. world, I-U declines to levels below the projections made in *NCMP 1973*.

For iron ore itself the Tables and Figures reveal the patterns of steel, more or less. If anything, they conform in even greater measure to the generalized description of the I-U pattern. In a few parts of the world during the period 1951-1975, direct use of pig iron was important (China, India, Brazil, Eastern Europe, U.S.S.R., for example). But the record is not a complete one and such use has certainly been of declining importance compared to the use of iron in steel production. The data here include the demand for such direct use insofar as information was available. For the most part, however, iron ore is integral to steel production. Its I-U estimates are essentially derived from the forces of demand, substitution/displacement and technological change in the world steel economy.

Ferroalloys

Specific consideration is given here to nickel, manganese, chromite, cobalt and tungsten, five of the most important additive materials in steel production. More than 70 percent of total consumption of each of these five is in the steel-making process; in the case of nickel and manganese, steel uses more than 90 percent of the total; only tungsten and cobalt find demands, in chemicals and carbides mostly, which in any way offer important competition with their availability for steel. It is understandable therefore that the I-U patterns for each of these materials conform to those revealed above for iron and steel. But some actual differences are significant.

The basic fact is that these additives provide special qualities (hardening, heat, stain, corrosion-resistance: "superalloys") that have only in recent decades become integral to the modern steel-making process. Their use-patterns are influenced by the extent of modernization of a region's steel industry and by the state of sophistication of its end-products. Demand for each additive is at a stage further removed from final product than is demand for steel proper. Such derived demand means that substitution possibilities are more readily implemented even when the additives constitute a very small ratio of total steel cost. Each of the five alloys can make some unique contribution to quality steels; yet substitution is widespread among the five as well as with other alloys—molybdenum and titanium, for example. Most major consuming regions depend heavily upon foreign imports of ferroalloys and tend therefore to be very alert to substitution possibilities for economic and technical reasons.

In sum, the I-U pattern for ferroalloys is less directly dependent upon the final goods demand force so important in steel and other materials. It is much more dependent on the substitution and technological forces relevant to I-U change. Peak intensities for these alloy materials occur at other times than for steel; future I-U levels can be expected to diverge from those in iron and steel proper. Relevant also is the fact that ferroalloy demand is related more closely to steel *production* than to total steel use. Ordinarily steel imports, particularly for rich lands like the U.S., are already "superalloyed"; such embodied alloys are not counted in apparent consumption of the alloy by the importing nation. On this account too the intensity patterns of alloys and steel can be expected to differ.

One final technical point is noted in this regard. The I-U patterns may at times be influenced by difficulties of demand measurement. Data on ferroalloy consumption are not readily assembled, and notably so for manganese, chromite and cobalt. "Apparent consumption" requires data for foreign trade as well as regional production, and both activities are measured in a variety of forms with differing metal and ore content. Standardization of materials consumption has yet to be extensively achieved in available statistics. Information here was assembled and standardized for metal content by various estimating devices. The resulting "apparent consumption" or demand is less tested and reliable for some alloys than are statistics for other important materials in this study. In particular, I-U levels and variations due to stockpile and inventory changes are hard to take into account.

Basic I-U data, including projections to 1985 and 2000, are shown for each of these alloys in Tables 4-3 through 4-7. These levels are related to per capita GDP in Figures 4-3 through 4-7. Following are supplementary observations on individual alloy materials.

Nickel (3)

By and large, intensities for this metal peak in very recent years in the developed nations of the world. Nickel is used in steel products purchased by industries of very high technological sophistication, notably in aerospace, petroleum and chemicals, where extreme heat and corrosion pose major problems. Given these technological needs, intensities will continue to remain at high levels, particularly in contrast to the downward movement in steel as a whole. In addition, new opportunities for use of nickel in desalinization may offer new markets. By and large, poor-nation nickel intensities are relatively low but they are expanding consistently as new steel enterprises are undertaken. One area of uncertainty for nickel involves the very high energy content of the smelting process now in use. Substitution possibilities may therefore lower the I-U projections below those shown. For the nickel statistics of Table 4-3 limitations of data necessitated the combination of three regions: U.S.S.R., Eastern Europe, and China. No breakdown could be presented for the rich nation-poor nation division of the world.

Manganese Ore (4)

This raw material is related fairly directly to steel because there are few substitution alternatives that are competitive to manganese for counteracting the sulphur content of iron in order to increase the malleability of crude steel. However, technological changes in steel are relevant here. Open-hearth steelmaking processes tend to use significantly larger amounts of manganese than do alternative processes. As the world steel industry has moved toward the basic oxygen process and to the electric furnace for steelmaking, manganese I-U levels have tended to be lowered: see Table 4-4 and Figure 4-4. The very high intensity figures for the U.S.S.R. may reflect the continuation there of open-hearth operations well beyond the time of shifts from open-hearth furnaces in the rich western nations. Also, the U.S.S.R. I-U data pose problems of inventory accumulation and strategic stockpiling for which correction could not be made with available data. This matter is significant since the U.S.S.R. is the largest single manganese producing world region. Increasing intensities in the poor nations reflect the role of special steels in their expanding output and in their programs for further growth. Gradually the non-steel use of manganese can also be expected to increase because of its importance in standard products where output is elastic with respect to income growth—such as batteries, photographical chemicals, tiles, bricks, fertilizers. Thus, and especially in the U.S., expansion of non-steel related demand for manganese provides some counter to other forces contributing to I-U decline. Over the long run, use of

Table 4-3
Intensity-of-Use: Nickel, 1951-2000
(metric tons per billion $ GDP, 1971 prices)

Region	1951-55	1961-65	1971-75	1985	2000
1. W. Europe	135.4	167.5	181.1	175.0	155.0
2. Japan	100.7	233.6	377.4	355.0	315.0
3. ODL*	48.0	75.0	101.1	95.0	85.0
4. U.S.S.R., China &					
E. Europe	NA	173.3	161.4	157.0	135.0
5. (See 4)					
6. Africa	3.9	16.0	49.4	55.0	50.0
7. Asia	4.0	13.2	18.2	25.0	30.0
8. L. America	5.4	10.6	33.7	40.0	45.0
9. (See 4)					
10. U.S.	124.4	157.9	143.1	125.0	105.0
Totals					
11. World	NA	147.0	156.1	149.2	134.2
12. Non-U.S. World	NA	142.0	161.3	158.5	145.2

Source: Appendix Table IV-3; also see text Chapter IV.

    * South Africa included with Africa (6).

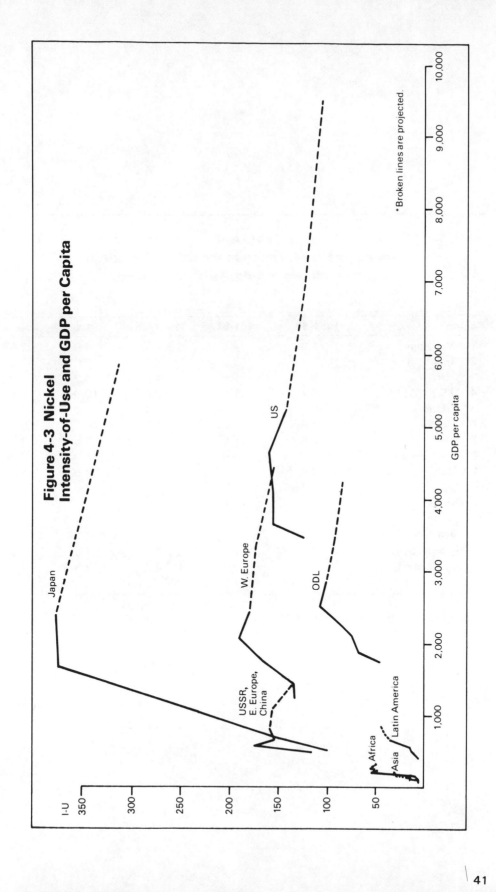

**Figure 4-3 Nickel
Intensity-of-Use and GDP per Capita**

I-U

Japan

USSR,
E. Europe, China

W. Europe

US

ODL

Africa

Asia

Latin America

GDP per capita

* Broken lines are projected.

Table 4-4
Intensity-of-Use: Manganese Ore, 1951-2000
(1000 metric tons per billion $ GDP, 1971 prices)

Region	1951-55	1961-65	1971-75	1985	2000
1. W. Europe	4.2	4.4	4.4	4.0	3.8
2. Japan	7.7	7.5	6.5	6.0	5.5
3. ODL	5.8	5.6	4.3	4.2	3.9
4. U.S.S.R.	15.7	15.2	10.4	10.0	9.5
5. E. Europe	8.2	7.8	5.1	5.0	4.8
6. Africa	3.8	4.9	6.7	7.5	8.5
7. Asia	2.4	5.6	6.9	7.5	8.0
8. L. America	2.7	6.0	5.4	6.0	7.0
9. China	2.8	11.0	7.0	7.5	9.0
10. U.S.	3.2	2.5	1.7	1.3	1.0
Totals					
11. World	5.5	6.2	5.1	4.9	4.8
12. Non-U.S. World	6.8	7.9	6.5	6.2	6.2
13. Poor Nations	2.7	6.9	6.4	7.0	7.9
14. Rich Nations	6.0	6.1	4.8	4.5	4.2

Source: Appendix Table IV-4; also see text, Chapter IV.

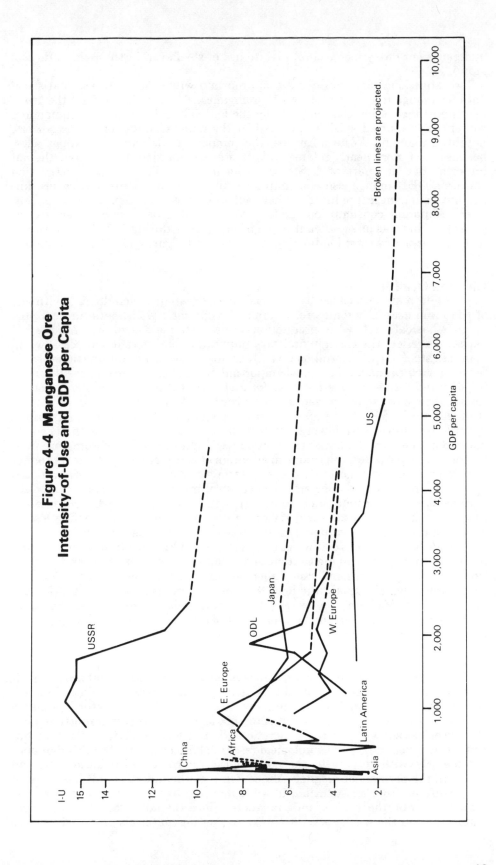

**Figure 4-4 Manganese Ore
Intensity-of-Use and GDP per Capita**

USSR

E. Europe

ODL

Japan

China

Africa

W. Europe

Latin America

Asia

US

*Broken lines are projected.

GDP per capita

I-U
15
14
12
10
8
6
4
2

1,000 2,000 3,000 4,000 5,000 6,000 7,000 8,000 9,000 10,000

43

manganese ore may increase relative to use of steel even in the rich lands as a group.

Two additional observations are appropriate with respect to the statistical data for manganese. One is that U.S. manganese demand data reflect the growing importance of net steel imports by the U.S. The relatively high manganese content of imported steel is included in the demand data for the exporters, notably Japan and Western Europe. U.S. manganese demand thus appears low because it is more nearly related to U.S. steel production, i.e. without the net imports that are part of U.S. steel consumption. The second observation concerns ODL manganese consumption. Australia and South Africa are important manganese producers. Their exports have been depressed in recent years. Apparent consumption tends to be overstated because of inventory expansion. This was of significant enough importance during 1971-75 to justify a (preliminary) downward adjustment of demand figures for these developed lands.

Chrome Ore (5)

These data are influenced by two basic considerations, each dealing with one of the main uses of chrome ore. Demand for chrome ore for metallurgical purposes is basically related to production levels of stainless steel. Most of the I-U variations reflect the changing relative importance of different sources of world stainless steel output as well as a vastly changed pattern of international trade flows in such products. The most important technological development affecting demand for use of this material for metallurgical purposes is the introduction of the new argon-oxygen-decarbonization (AOD) process for producing stainless steel. With this process, purity of stainless steel can be maintained despite use of ores with lower ferrochromite content; this reduces the need for chrome ore per ton of stainless steel produced. With regard to chrome ore used for refractory purposes, the trends in adoption of new techniques of steel production in general are important; the long-term worldwide shift away from open-hearth to oxygen and electric furnace steel-making has served to reduce chrome ore I-U. Despite such forces to reduce chrome ore I-U, chrome ore intensities in the various world regions are expected on net to decline less or expand more over the next decades than was the case during 1951-75.

The specific materials estimates of Table 4-5 and Figure 4-5 were constructed by standardizing the chrome content in available statistics on trade and production for a range of chrome-containing metals and products. In addition, the same factors which explain the low U.S. figures for manganese consumption apply in the case of chrome ore as well: the U.S. has ceded its former pre-eminence as a stainless steel producer to Japan and Western Europe. It now imports a large part of its requirements from these regions.

Cobalt (6)

This metal and in some measure tungsten have I-U patterns that are less intimately related to steel patterns than was true for the preceding alloys. In addition to its special qualities in making steel for high-temperature products ("superalloys" for jet engines and rotor blades) cobalt serves important non-steel uses associated with the magnetic and chemical properties of the metal. Extensive investment in technological research has contributed to this demand, particularly with respect to the combination of cobalt with aluminum and nickel in the permanent magnet, Alnico. On the other hand, cobalt has increasingly suffered from substitution, in some measure by nickel but mostly by the growth in importance of ceramic magnets. Since the late 1950s, technological change has on the whole served to make competing materials progressively less

44

Table 4-5

Intensity-of-Use: Chrome Ore, 1951-2000

(metric tons per billion $ GDP, 1971 prices)

Region	1951-55	1961-65	1971-75	1985	2000
1. W. Europe	1848	1785	2000	2100	2000
2. Japan	1731	3619	4372	4260	4150
3. ODL	3203	2304	4033	4100	4200
4. U.S.S.R.	1525	1270	1215	900	700
5. E. Europe	2095	2500	3282	3500	3500
6. Africa	344	416	686	750	800
7. Asia	390	434	913	1000	1100
8. L. America	180	188	544	700	800
9. China	226	690	1504	1700	1800
10. U.S.	2030	1536	1024	735	500
Totals					
11. World	1713	1568	1753	1692	1609
12. Non-U.S. World	1542	1582	2041	2060	2025
13. Poor Nations	280	414	905	1035	1122
14. Rich Nations	1957	1763	1909	1814	1700

Source: Appendix Table IV-5; also see text, Chapter IV.

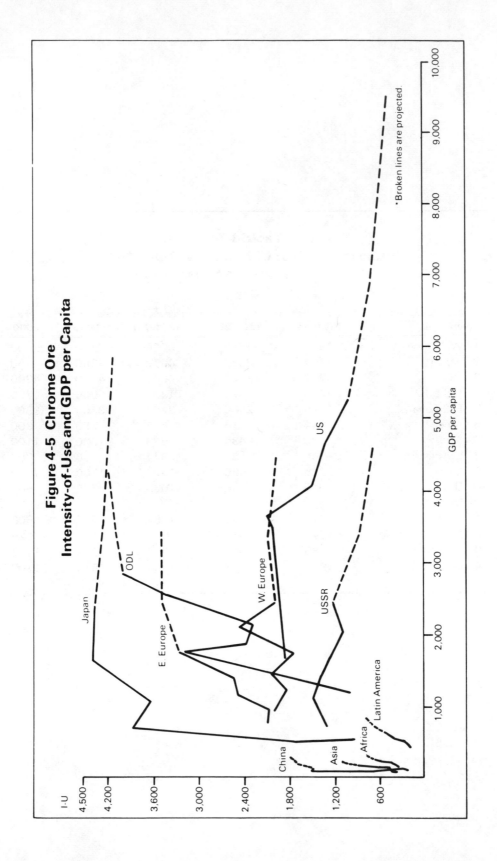

**Figure 4-5 Chrome Ore
Intensity-of-Use and GDP per Capita**

I-U

US

ODL

Japan

W Europe

E Europe

USSR

Latin America

China

Asia

Africa

GDP per capita

*Broken lines are projected.

4,500
4,200
3,600
3,000
2,400
1,800
1,200
600

1,000   2,000   3,000   4,000   5,000   6,000   7,000   8,000   9,000   10,000

Table 4-6

Intensity-of-Use: Cobalt, 1951-2000

(metric tons per billion $ GDP, 1971 prices)

Region	1951-55	1961-65	1971-75	1985	2000
1. W. Europe	6.4	9.5	6.5	6.2	5.6
2. Japan	5.9	14.7	15.3	14.8	13.8
3. ODL	6.7	9.6	8.2	8.0	7.6
4. U.S.S.R.	2.0	2.4	3.2	3.2	3.0
5. E. Europe	5.0	6.3	4.9	5.0	4.7
6. Africa	13.2	12.0	9.9	10.5	11.0
7. Asia	0.1	0.6	1.3	2.8	3.6
8. L. America	1.3	0.9	1.7	2.8	3.6
9. China	0.3	0.5	1.4	2.0	3.2
10. U.S.	7.9	6.5	6.5	6.4	6.0
Totals					
11. World	5.6	6.0	5.9	6.0	5.8
12. Non-U.S. World	4.4	5.8	5.7	5.8	5.7
13. Poor Nations	2.0	2.0	2.4	3.5	4.4
14. Rich Nations	6.3	6.7	6.6	6.4	6.1

Source: Appendix Table IV-6; also see text, Chapter IV.

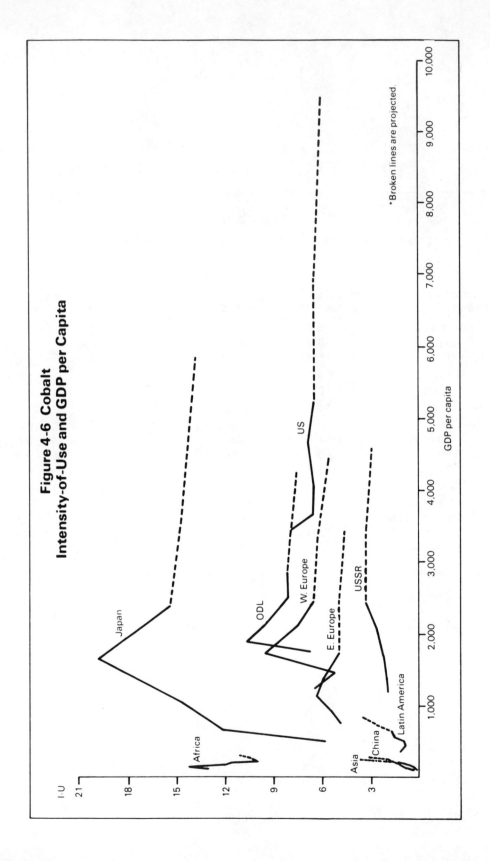

Figure 4-6 Cobalt
Intensity-of-Use and GDP per Capita

*Broken lines are projected.

GDP per capita

I-U

48

costly than cobalt. The I-U patterns for cobalt in Table 4-6 correspond closely with the general considerations discussed in the opening section of Chapter IV. Data for Africa again reflect inventory adjustment difficulties; about 80 percent of all cobalt is produced in Africa as defined here, i.e. excluding South Africa. For Japan, high intensities are again interpreted principally as a consequence of Japan's exports of goods containing cobalt.

Tungsten (7)

Tungsten has long played a dominant role for cutting tools, whether in high speed steel, non-ferrous alloys or tungsten carbides. All are of fundamental importance in metalworking machinery, construction, mining and transportation equipment. The use of tungsten is thus heavily influenced by modernization and by the development of heavy industry. Over the years from 1951, growth rates of tungsten use have kept abreast of GDP growth, but the growth rate was higher in the poor nations. Not only were steel intensities declining in the rich world, but molybdenum (a mineral with properties discovered from pointed technological research investigations) made deep inroads into tungsten use for cutting tools, a substitution that apparently benefited more from relative cost advantages than from the metal's technical advantages for high-speed steel manufacture. The outlook for the world, the non-U.S. world and the rich nations is for declining levels of I-U; steady upward movement is anticipated in the I-U of poor lands.

Tungsten data have been carefully studied by the U.N., especially for the years since 1960 and for Japan and the rich nations of the West. The presentation here of world and other regional data again required some standardization of ores for tungsten content. The data for China, which serve also to explain the high average I-U levels for the poor nations as a group, probably reflect inventory accumulations from China's large production, as well as high rates of industrial utilization per unit of GDP. For China does use large amounts of tungsten in its steel program. On the whole, the U.S.S.R., Eastern Europe and China show a much smaller response to the advantages that serve molybdenum in the western world. The technical superiority of tungsten for high-speed steel is broadly accepted. The neglect of molybdenum probably reflects differences in cost structure for these substitute metals in major tungsten-producing centers in a non-market system.

Refined Copper (8)

The intensity-of-use data for copper embody most of the general propositions of Chapter IV. Demand factors serve to explain upward movement followed by downward movement in the rich nations; they permit ready interpretation of the fairly steady upward trend in intensities for the poor lands. Between 1951-55 and 1971-75, I-U levels more than doubled in the poor nations as a group. For the rich lands, and for the world and non-U.S. world, I-U has increased to a peak and decreased over these same years. Current trends bid fair to continue (Table 4-8; Figure 4-8). Modernization of economies and significant GDP growth mean more need for copper. In particular, such activities as construction, electrical generation and transmission, and communications which make heavy use of copper, feature large in the development process.

There have been significant technological developments in copper, notably in the ore extraction stage. Essentially it was improvements in mining technology that permitted some offset to the price increases associated with decreasing metal content of the average ton mined since 1951. Moreover there has been some progress in the technology of processing: continuous casting, semicontinuous casting, continuous smelting. While these have tended to reduce

Table 4-7
Intensity-of-Use: Tungsten, 1951-2000
(metric tons per billion $ GDP, 1971 prices)

Region	1951-55	1961-65	1971-75	1985	2000
1. W. Europe	13.3	14.0	12.4	12.0	11.0
2. Japan	11.3	19.5	10.7	10.0	9.0
3. ODL	1.4	3.1	3.2	3.0	2.8
4. U.S.S.R.	17.1	14.2	10.8	10.0	9.5
5. E. Europe	12.7	15.3	16.9	17.0	16.5
6. Africa	2.3	1.7	9.6	10.0	10.2
7. Asia	5.6	4.5	4.2	5.0	6.0
8. L. America	8.4	2.5	6.9	8.0	9.0
9. China	37.4	43.4	37.5	39.0	40.0
10. U.S.	6.6	7.3	5.8	5.0	4.5
Totals					
11. World	11.0	11.5	10.2	9.9	9.5
12. Non-U.S. World	13.4	13.5	14.9	11.8	11.3
13. Poor Nations	14.5	12.6	13.5	14.6	15.3
14. Rich Nations	10.4	11.4	9.5	9.1	8.4

Source: Appendix Table IV-7; also see text, Chapter IV.

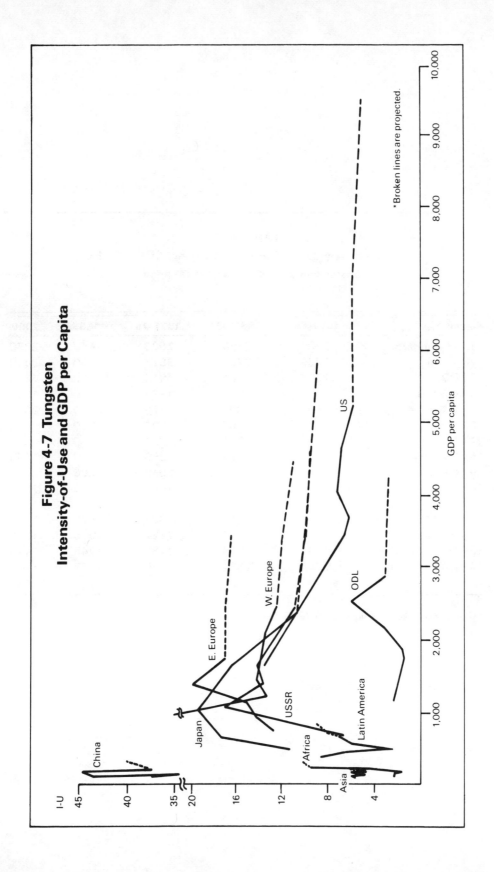

**Figure 4-7 Tungsten
Intensity-of-Use and GDP per Capita**

* Broken lines are projected.

Table 4-8
Intensity-of-Use: Refined Copper, 1951-2000
(metric tons per billion $ GDP, 1971 prices)

Region	1951-55	1961-65	1971-75	1985	2000
1. W. Europe	2937	3193	2586	2450	2350
2. Japan	2239	3789	3577	3150	2800
3. ODL	2314	3004	1944	1900	1600
4. U.S.S.R.	1839	1906	1777	1500	1350
5. E. Europe	1697	2008	2379	2200	2050
6. Africa	218	267	291	350	400
7. Asia	452	812	551	600	650
8. L. America	1176	1121	1389	1500	1650
9. China	123	1310	2019	2200	2750
10. U.S.	2330	2174	1681	1550	1200
Totals					
11. World	2116	2295	2001	1870	1720
12. Non-U.S. World	2010	2349	2127	1995	1915
13. Poor Nations	546	959	1135	1245	1445
14. Rich Nations	2384	2521	2160	1985	1770

Source: Appendix Table IV-8; also see text, Chapter IV.

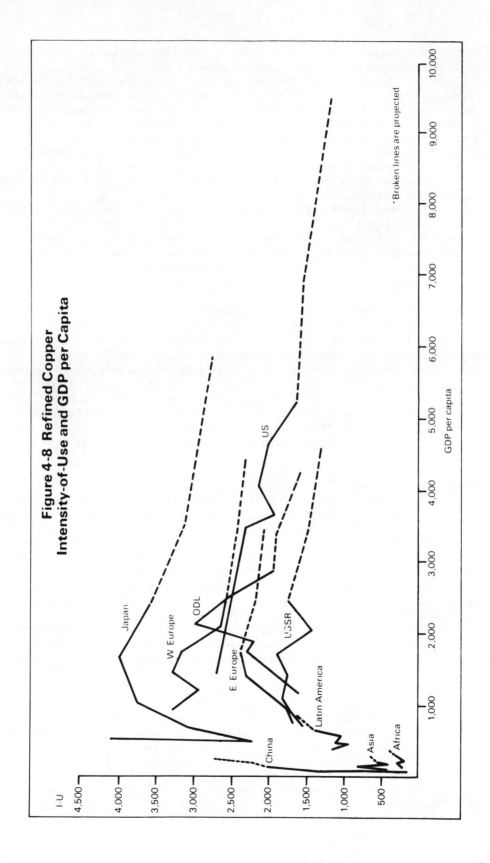

Figure 4-8 Refined Copper
Intensity-of-Use and GDP per Capita

I-U

4,500

4,000

3,500

3,000

2,500

2,000

1,500

1,000

500

GDP per capita

1,000   2,000   3,000   4,000   5,000   6,000   7,000   8,000   9,000   10,000

Japan

W Europe

ODL

E Europe

US

USSR

Latin America

China

Asia

Africa

·Broken lines are projected

production costs per unit of copper, it is not clear that they have had much influence on reducing copper inputs per unit of final goods.

The use of copper in rich lands has been affected mostly by the substitution potential of other metals, notably aluminum, for use in producer durables, construction, motor vehicles and especially in electrical transmission. This last accounted for about one-half of all copper use in recent decades; it is here where aluminum has substituted for important uses of copper. Technological development of the solid conductor, of microminiaturization of communications circuits, of satellite relays and of nuclear power has served to favor the substitution of aluminum for copper. For the most part, these displacements are irreversible in a given installation.

Further substitution by aluminum may be expected in the future, arising from the interplay of relative price developments and differences in income elasticities. Aluminum elasticities have tended to be higher. In the U.S. especially, substitution of aluminum for copper has moved relatively more rapidly than in other regions, even though relative price differences between competing materials have remained roughly in line among regions. This augurs for more substitution as other regions move to higher income levels.

On the other side the data available after *NCMP 1973* suggest some slowing down of the copper intensity declines noted earlier. Prices of aluminum and plastics (used for insulation for aluminum in electrical transmission) have been adversely affected by energy and especially petroleum costs. In any event, for these and perhaps other reasons not yet clear, copper use seems to have become less prone to substitution. As Table 4-8 indicates, I-U declines in rich lands are moderate. There has been less decline than projected in 1973 for example. There is as yet little evidence of rapid shifts away from copper that would impede the growing I-U's of poor lands shown in Table 4-8. For the world as a whole, the declines in I-U persist but I-U's remain somewhat above the levels anticipated for 2000 a few years back.

Primary Aluminum (9)

The record and the prospect for the intensity-of-use of this metal remain clear. There is no evidence of an absolute decline anywhere, although rates of growth have become persistently lower in the main consuming regions. This slackening now appears more marked than was anticipated earlier. World, non-U.S. world, rich nation levels are now expected to be lower in 2000 than were projected in *NCMP 1973;* poor nation I-U's are seen as somewhat higher. The observations above with regard to the copper prospect and especially the uncertain price prospect for aluminum over the next decades of energy shortage are consistent with the outlook in Table 4-9 and Figure 4-9.

There remains an impressive and widening technical scope for further displacement by aluminum for iron ore, nickel, tin and zinc in metal production, and for steel and copper metal goods. Mention has already been made of the expanding role of aluminum in electrical transmission. Construction and transportation equipment (automobiles particularly) and an expanding array of consumer goods have become ever greater users of aluminum in most parts of the world. The rapid growth in I-U in poor lands combines a high income effect as the economies develop (or at least industrialize), supplemented by what is generally a positive substitution effect. For the rich world negative income effects are more than offset by substitution. It is hard to visualize a turning point for the I-U and GDP per capita relationship of Figure 4-9. Currently relative price developments, some of which have become manifest over brief periods in special product situations, seem to be key to any broad movement away from high levels of I-U for aluminum over the next decades.

Platinum-Group Metals (10)

Data do not permit comprehensive time coverage of use of these metals on a world basis. Appendix Table IV-10 reveals a pattern of intensity more similar to aluminum than to other materials in this study. But the present analysis anticipates an I-U prospect different from the aluminum case. Despite significant increases in the five-year averages from 1951, a turn-around seems actually to have occurred in many rich nations. The U.S., Western Europe and Other Developed Lands are expected to have somewhat reduced I-U levels by 1985 with substantial further reductions by 2000. Similar developments are considered probable after 1985 in Eastern Europe and the U.S.S.R. For Japan and the poor nations, continued expansion in intensity is foreseen, although growth rates will be lower for Japan, China and perhaps for other developing lands.

The most striking aspect of the record is of course the extraordinary level of use-intensity in Japan after the postwar reconstruction and development effort of the 1950s. Since 1951 the annual average growth rate of demand for this metal in Japan exceeded 25 percent, as against a growth rate below 10 percent for GDP. Seventy percent of Japan's total is for use of platinum metal in jewelry, in contrast to well under 3 percent for such purposes in the U.S., where I-U has maintained high levels, although well below Japan's. In most industrialized and rich nations the platinum-group of metals has actually found important uses for an increasing array of high technology purposes in industry because of the metals' unusual catalytic properties. Over the past decades they have become important in chemicals for plastics, synthetic rubber, pesticides, nitrogenous fertilizers, and in explosives. Their role in catalytic converters for controlling automotive emissions raised converter use to over a third of U.S. total use in 1974, the first year of such application.

This growing demand effect, manifest in poor nations as well as in the rich, is encountering some offsets from expanding efforts to develop substitute sources with these catalytic properties. With the cost of platinum in excess of $200 per troy ounce, catalysts with nickel, tungsten, chromium, cobalt, molybdenum and silver have been developed within recent years. These did permit some shifts from the platinum group in many chemicals, and in some degree in electrical devices and in the glass industry. The catalysts are less efficient but they are economically advantageous. More decisive for platinum I-U over the longer period is the prospective development of entirely different emission control devices. Such processes as charge stratification and electronic control may well take over this major automotive demand by the year 2000. Therefore, I-U estimates have been lowered for that date. This effect will of course encompass Japan's future industrial use of the platinum metals—but it is not likely to affect demand for platinum jewelry in that country.

Zinc (11)

Significant changes have been made in I-U patterns and levels for zinc since *NCMP 1973*, basically because additional (and new sources of) information now permit a much more comprehensive account of the historical use patterns. Of course the underlying relationships found in most other materials continue to prevail in zinc with respect both to the reduced pressure of demand as developed nations become wealthier, and the steady expansion in poor nations as their economies modernize. In the early 1970s, use of zinc to galvanize steel was still growing relative to GDP in many rich countries, although no longer in the U.S. and Japan. The role of zinc in a broad range of anti-corrosion uses continued to acquire technical and economic (relative cost) gains. The vigor of this development has prompted an intensity level for 2000 in the non-U.S. world that is

Table 4-9
Intensity-of-Use: Primary Aluminum, 1951-2000
(metric tons per billion $ GDP, 1971 prices)

Region	1951-55	1961-65	1971-75	1985	2000
1. W. Europe	1565	2283	3056	3300	3500
2. Japan	866	2258	4863	5600	6000
3. ODL	1287	1803	2876	3200	3500
4. U.S.S.R.	1363	2106	2413	2450	2500
5. E. Europe	876	2247	3647	3750	4200
6. Africa	37	163	559	600	900
7. Asia	140	764	1462	1500	1850
8. L. America	369	879	1656	1900	2300
9. China	44	1033	1630	1950	2350
10. U.S.	2174	3002	3911	4400	4900
Totals					
11. World	1478	2239	3093	3397	3730
12. Non-U.S. World	1103	1892	2770	3011	3292
13. Poor Nations	169	791	1461	1635	2009
14. Rich Nations	1702	2485	3394	3722	4051

Source: Appendix Table IV-9; also see text, Chapter IV.

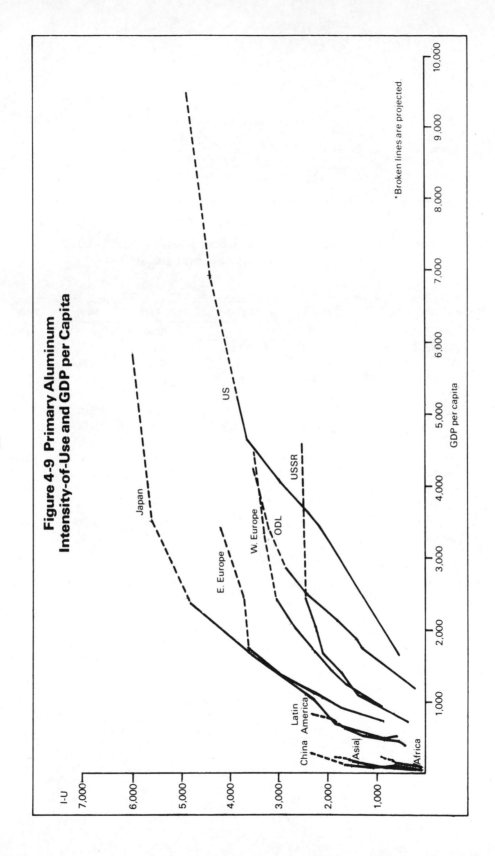

Figure 4-9 Primary Aluminum
Intensity-of-Use and GDP per Capita

*Broken lines are projected.

Table 4-10

Intensity-of-Use: Platinum-Group Metals, 1951-2000

(troy ounces per billion $ GDP, 1971 prices)

Region	1951-55	1961-65	1971-75*	1985	2000
1. W. Europe	388	676	698	675	625
2. Japan	411	3151	6847	7300	7400
3. ODL†	499	1425	1480	1450	1400
4. U.S.S.R. & E. Europe	NA	582	831	925	875
6. Africa	11	95	534	600	725
7. Asia	61	170	698	800	875
8. L. America	191	165	170	250	300
9. China†	NA	95	856	950	975
10. U.S.	1035	1293	1479	1450	1250
Totals					
11. World	NA	906	1360	1444	1433
12. Non-U.S. World	NA	730	1313	1442	1502
13. Poor Nations	NA	142	545	629	682
14. Rich Nations	NA	1036	1511	1595	1573

Source: Appendix Table IV-10; also see text, Chapter IV

†Historical data approximate.

* Preliminary; in particular regions (3)-(9) based on 1971-73 approximations.

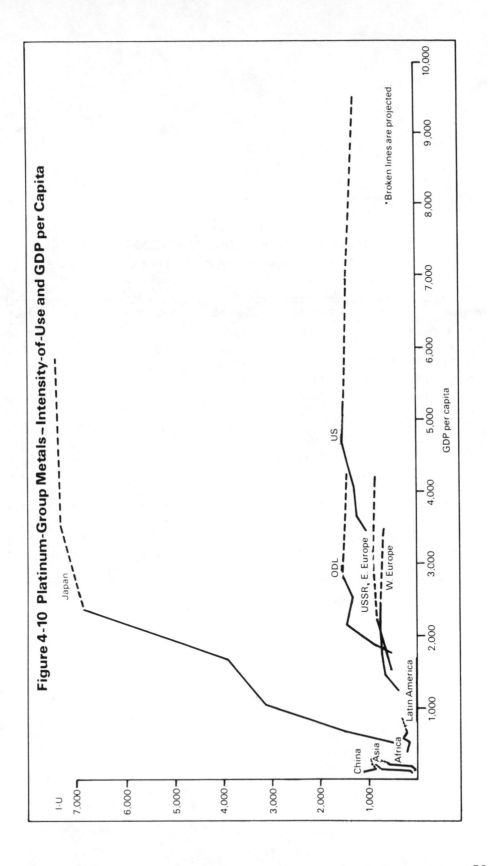

Figure 4-10 Platinum-Group Metals–Intensity-of-Use and GDP per Capita

*Broken lines are projected.

Table 4-11
Intensity-of-Use: Zinc, 1951-2000
(metric tons per billion $ GDP, 1971 prices)

Region	1951-55	1961-65	1971-75	1985	2000
1. W. Europe	1909	1941	1661	1550	1400
2. Japan	1902	2926	2612	2400	1850
3. ODL	1673	1816	1724	1650	1575
4. U.S.S.R.	1110	1011	1348	1350	1250
5. E. Europe	1390	1850	1995	1750	1650
6. Africa	23	122	328	350	400
7. Asia	367	956	1042	1150	1200
8. L. America	699	867	1129	1200	1300
9. China	94	1119	1323	1350	1500
10. U.S.	1550	1312	1034	950	750
Totals					
11. World	1408	1440	1391	1364	1228
12. Non-U.S. World	1332	1497	1532	1520	1407
13. Poor Nations	328	630	1052	1120	1211
14. Rich Nations	1592	1577	1492	1406	1231

Source: Appendix Table IV-11; also see text, Chapter IV.

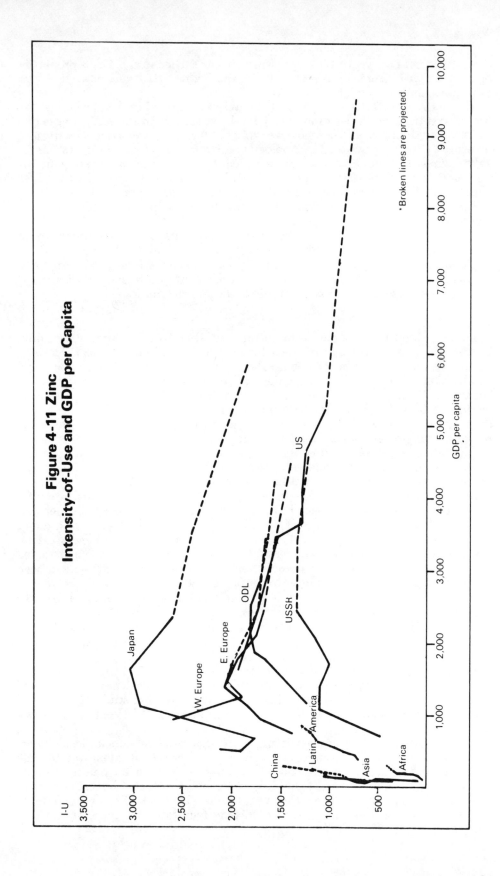

**Figure 4-11 Zinc
Intensity-of-Use and GDP per Capita**

I-U

*Broken lines are projected.

GDP per capita

some 10 percent above the figure presented in the earlier study. These properties of zinc are also primarily responsible for the higher I-U levels now shown for most poor lands.

The many uses for zinc in die-casting and in brass and bronze products also provided a positive thrust to intensity levels, especially in the early stages of a society's modernization. Here however zinc has fared less well from substitution pressures than its price and technological advantages permitted in its use for galvanizing. Aluminum has made significant inroads into die-casting in the automotive industry (the largest single end-use for this purpose in the U.S., Japan and Western European countries). Magnesium seems to be playing a comparable role in reducing the scope for zinc in the castings for modern aircraft engines.

Table 4-11 and Figure 4-11 document I-U patterns that have already been well established in most of the materials discussed above. World, non-U.S. world and rich nation intensities are moving downward fairly steadily and particularly in the U.S. and Japan. Poor lands continue to show increasing I-U's, many at absolute levels comparable to those of rich nations.

Tin (12)

Table 4-12 for tin provides an important variation from the preceding tables in this series: the "poor-nation" data for past periods (line 13) reflect the *same* expansion-contraction pattern as do the data for the other three major world subdivisions on that Table, and indeed as in practically all the rich regions of the world. By the decade of the 1950's, and before that time in most parts of the world, the tin industry had gone through a major technological change: the shift from hot-dipping to electrolytic tinplating processes. In itself this was a tin metal-saving process, which rapidly became the almost universal process for the production of tinplate, the predominant use to which the tin metal is put. This meant that developing nations were unlikely to experience the high intensity-of-use stage that most rich lands had earlier been through in tin.

In some measure this tin I-U experience, 1951-75, provides documentation for a phenomenon that was present but not very visible in the record of other materials in this study. In the case of tin, the role of technical change was a major determinant of the intensity-of-use pattern. I-U variations in other industrial raw materials have usually been dominated by forces stemming from a changing and expanding GDP. There is no question that technological change has been widespread: in the case of preceding minerals note was taken of the role of technology in I-U change. But tin is the only case studied in which a decisive technological breakthrough may well have dominated the world picture for intensity, in poor as well as in rich lands. In contrast for example, the shift from open hearth steel-making did affect the input per unit of output of a range of alloys, but these important effects were on the whole submerged by GDP-associated forces. In the present study there is thus provided firm evidence for what could only be hypothesized in the 1973 work. Further documentation and analysis can fill an essential need. There is scope for further study in tin as well as in other minerals in the search for greater knowledge of I-U behavior for raw materials inputs.

Figure 4-12 more than any earlier figure in this series reflects a decisive narrowing of world I-U's measured at levels of per capita GDP along the income axis. Table 4-12 reflects narrowing of regional I-U's at given points of time. These changes are functions of the widespread effect of technological change in the tin-using industries, given the types of uses that tin fills throughout the world. Narrowing over time and over income facilitates the projection of I-U levels to 1985 and 2000.

Table 4-12
Intensity-of-Use: Tin, 1951-2000
(metric tons per billion $ GDP, 1971 prices)

Region	1951-55	1961-65	1971-75	1985	2000
1. W. Europe	139.5	112.3	73.5	60	50
2. Japan	128.0	159.4	127.1	110	100
3. ODL	113.5	98.1	64.4	55	50
4. U.S.S.R.	61.8	67.3	29.8	25	20
5. E. Europe	70.6	65.6	76.6	65	55
6. Africa	46.6	38.8	24.9	60	55
7. Asia	60.8	52.9	37.8	35	30
8. L. America	69.1	53.9	36.5	35	30
9. China	33.5	156.0	100.8	90	80
10. U.S.	100.5	72.7	46.8	35	25
Totals					
11. World	97.9	86.3	58.8	50	40
12. Non-U.S. World	96.6	92.4	63.5	55	46
13. Poor Nations	54.3	75.4	50.6	52	44
14. Rich Nations	105.4	88.1	60.3	49	39

Source: Appendix Table IV-12; also see text, Chapter IV.

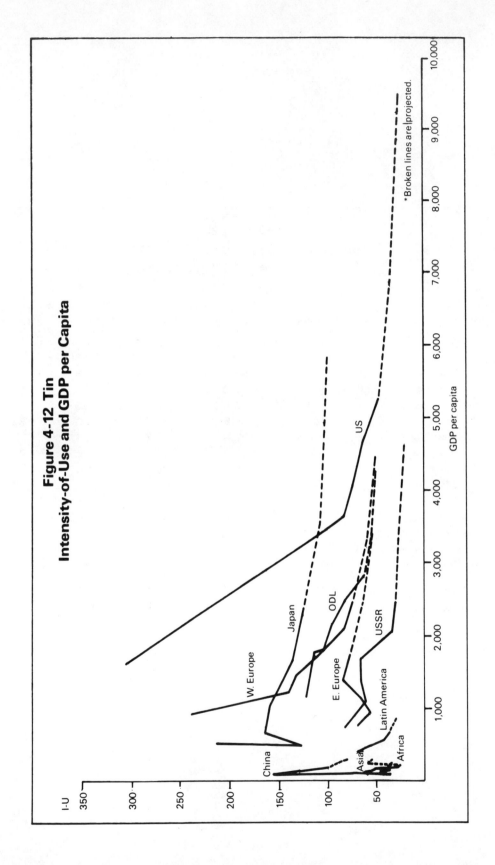

Figure 4-12 Tin
Intensity-of-Use and GDP per Capita

*Broken lines are projected.

GDP per capita

I-U

US
Japan
ODL
USSR
W. Europe
E. Europe
Latin America
China
Asia
Africa

Summary Observations

For all the materials considered here, the Tables and Figures provide support for the reality of patterns in I-U behavior, albeit at different levels in different regions. There has been no comprehensive identification of specific magnitudes of intensity shifts due to technological change or to substitution associated with price and policy changes. The fundamental force in I-U level probably remains the level of production of goods and services relative to population; technological progress probably does serve to narrow regional I-U differences. At least this last pertains within limits set by specialized production and trade activities in a region. As illustrated earlier, limits arise from the fact that apparent consumption levels of raw materials have only a partial relevance to a nation's per capita income. There is raw material "consumption" in imports of final goods and services. There are also important I-U effects in special national policies (e.g., military expansion). Such regional attributes warrant further study in an effort to improve I-U projections.

Substitution forces are enhanced by the indirect nature of demand for any particular input. Demand for material inputs is a derived demand, in contrast to the demand for final goods where consumer preferences are reflected directly. Thus, consumers are little if at all concerned with the specific metal that conducts their electricity, as an example; their use satisfactions are derived from the product which electricity serves. Also, the metal input component generally contributes a relatively small part to the value of the product directly demanded; variations in the raw materials price are not apt to have large influence on demand for the final product and therefore for the material input. Price elasticity of demand for specific inputs thus tends to be low, but substitutability among materials inputs tends to be high when there is any differential price behavior among actual substitutable materials. Such behavioral attributes enhance the effectiveness of the market (and of national policy) to influence the level and pattern of materials demand, important goals given the world's concern about materials shortages and resource limits. Indeed, policy options for materials obviously improve man's capacity to make the types of social and economic adaptations that could mitigate the dangers of minerals exhaustion. In terms of the methodological discussion of Chapter II, such substitution possibilities serve to support the critical role of human as against material inputs in the economic expansion process.

The combined influence of these income, technology and substitution factors has of course provided the declining world I-U reflected in most materials of this study. Such shifts in intensity, primarily in the direction of lowering the relative importance of the role that materials play in the course of economic development, have been well recorded in historical studies. The present answers on the outlook for intensity-of-use of raw materials suggest continuity with this past experience. Materials requirements promise to continue to become relatively less important inputs in the production of the final goods and services that the world seeks.

Chapter V
The Future Demand for Raw Materials

The combination of GDP and population (in GDP per person) with intensity-of-use measures, all as projected above for 1985 and for 2000, provides the answers of this study for future demand for each of the twelve raw materials considered here. The amount of each that the world, the non-U.S. world, the poor and the rich nations, as well as the ten regional components of the world, will use up in 1985 and in 2000 is given separately in Tables 5-1.1 through 5-1.12, along with some historical comparisons. All the past data assembled are available in the form of five-year averages in Appendix Tables V-1 through V-12. In Table 5a, which follows, total world and non-U.S. world demands are given for 1971-1975 and 2000, with the ratio that summarizes the expansion anticipated over these decades.

It is clear that the world can be expected to use some two to three times the volume of raw materials in a year at the end of the century than it used in the average year over a recent five year period. Actually, most ratios are below 2.5, and closer to 2.0. The non-U.S. world shows comparable results, usually with somewhat higher ratios because the U.S. itself tends to have relatively lower rates of future growth in materials demand than does the rest of the world.

These results contrast markedly with the data of *NCMP 1973*, where comparable ratios were reported "between three and four" (almost six for aluminum).[10] In terms of absolute tonnages, the end-century amounts for steel are *lower* by some 250 m.m.t. (84 percent of the 1973 estimate), iron in iron ore by over 165 m.m.t. (85 percent), refined copper by almost 3 m.m.t. (85 percent), primary aluminum by some 10 m.m.t. (88 percent), and zinc by well over 1 m.m.t. (89 percent). On the whole, *NCMP 1973* results were broadly recognized as being below the levels of other projections then available for the year 2000. Mostly such differences were due to the fact that other estimates had built into them the I-U levels of past experience, rather than the shifts in these past levels that are significant in a developing world. In any event, the present figures are very much below the range of other estimates available in the early 1970s.[11]

---

[10]*NCMP 1973*, pp. 20, 37.

[11]No comprehensive effort has been made to assemble alternative projections made or in progress over the past two or three years. For each material discussed here, a thorough survey preceded completion of the historical basis and the projected data. These did not uncover any comprehensive source of alternative published projections.

Table 5a
Demand for Raw Materials: Expansion, 1971-2000

		World			Non-U.S. World		
		1971-75	**2000**	**Ratio**	**1971-75**	**2000**	**Ratio**
Crude Steel	(m.m.t)	642	1301	2.0	507	1088	2.1
Iron Ore	(m.m.t)	432	919	2.1	346	786	2.3
Nickel	(t.m.t)	618	1314	2.1	458	1034	2.3
Manganese Ore	(t.m.t)	20030	46726	2.3	18101	44058	2.4
Chrome Ore	(t.m.t)	6941	15751	2.3	5792	14417	2.5
Cobalt	(m.t)	23434	56720	2.4	16152	40712	2.5
Tungsten	(m.t)	40182	92637	2.3	33672	80631	2.4
Refined Copper	(t.m.t)	7923	16839	2.1	6037	13637	2.3
Primary Aluminum	(t.m.t)	12249	36516	3.0	7861	23443	3.0
Platinum	(t.tr.oz.)	5387	14030	2.6	3726	10695	2.9
Zinc	(t.m.t)	5506	12022	2.2	4346	10021	2.3
Tin	(t.m.t)	232	393	1.7	180	326	1.8

The order of magnitude of the world's requirements for most of its industrial raw materials is thus now seen to be significantly lower at the end of the century than were the magnitudes earlier anticipated. The present analysis applied methods comparable to those in *NCMP 1973*. The results endorse the major thrust of the earlier effort: man and society were working toward reduced rates of materials utilization relative to the final goods and services they were striving to attain. The fact that the present data represent a 15 percent reduction from the 1973 projection must be attributed to a judgment on man's aspirations for progress and the skills he employs to that end. The fact cannot be attributed to the weight of imminent materials resource exhaustion or of environmental deterioration. As indicated earlier, present views of the year 2000 envisage world per capita GDP of some 50 percent above the 1971-75 levels in real terms (some 20 percent above by 1985). Consistently, total materials demand estimates involve the following conclusions with regard to the course of per capita utilization of industrial raw materials. These data pertain to the world as a whole. In no regional component is there any indication of actual declines in per capita use estimates over the next decades.

Table 5b
Materials Use per Capita, Total World: 1971-2000

		1971-75	1985	2000
Crude Steel	(kg)	166.9	182.3	204.6
Iron Ore	(kg)	112.2	126.5	144.4
Nickel	(g)	161.0	184.0	206.0
Manganese Ore	(kg)	5.3	6.1	7.6
Chrome Ore	(kg)	1.8	2.1	2.5
Cobalt	(g)	6.1	7.4	8.9
Tungsten	(g)	10.4	12.2	14.6
Refined Copper	(kg)	2.1	2.3	2.7
Primary Aluminum	(kg)	3.2	4.2	5.7
Platinum	(tr.oz/1000)	1.4	1.8	2.2
Zinc	(kg)	1.4	1.7	1.9
Tin	(g)	60.4	61.2	61.7

The full array of materials data is given in accompanying Tables 5-1.1 through 5-1.12, with the more complete record for 1951-1975 in Appendix Tables V-1 to V-12. These present the entire range of regional results. Broad generalizations show poor nation shares of world use expanding, albeit slowly. Among the rich lands the U.S. share of total world use continues to decline. The differential growth rate of demand in poor lands is less marked than it promised to be in the 1973 study. An important part of the explanation for this last may lie in the force of technological change. It appears now that poor nations expand their materials I-U along different paths than were relevant when today's rich lands were developing.

These demand data are also shown in terms of average annual rates of growth over the historical period, 1951-75, and the projected period, 1975-85 and 1975-2000, in Tables 5-2.1 through 5-2.12. For most materials future annual rates to 1985 as well as to 2000 tend to be some 40-60 percent of the average rates for 1951-75. Exceptions take the form of more limited declines—and even occasional increases, notably in the U.S.—in the case of alloy metals where technological developments in frontier areas have checked long declines in historical I-U's. These have been noted in Chapter IV above. On the whole, poor-nation growth rates in demand for raw materials continue to exceed the levels anticipated for the rich nations, and of course for the world as a whole.

Quite clearly, the Tables in the 5-2 series simply embody the changes discussed in I-U and in GDP. As indicated in Chapter IV, the broad expectation is for I-U to be higher in near future decades than it was in past decades for the poor nations; for the rich lands, the parallel expectation is for lower I-U's. For both together, i.e., for the entire world, I-U generally tends downward[12] because so large a proportion of total world use will long continue to occur in the wealthier lands. As indicated in Chapter III, future GDP growth rates are not expected to differ substantially in these two divisions of world nations. Hence the outlook is for higher materials demand growth rates in poor nations.

With respect to the relative importance of these two variables (GDP change and I-U change) in the demand change over time in any region, the role of GDP change as projected here is significantly larger than is the role of projected I-U change. Comparison of the 1973 and the present outlooks for the year 2000 suggested a 15 percent lower increase in materials demand on a total world basis: two-thirds may be due to the present study's altered GDP growth rates and one-third to its new I-U levels. These ratios do of course differ among regions and among materials.

Perhaps the only additional note necessary here on this matter is to recall that I-U behavior is very much what man and his society have made it. Moreover, reductions in I-U levels along an inverted-U pattern are a force that contributes to lower need for raw materials for a given level of final goods output. This force is beneficial to man and society. On the other hand, low rates of GDP growth are not beneficial, and especially not in the world's poor nations where live more than 70 percent of total world population. Accelerating GDP growth over the next decades is an important world objective. Such acceleration would certainly expand the rates of growth of demand for materials beyond those projected in the Tables of the 5-1 and 5-2 series. Such expansion would in turn generate the forces for movement to still lower I-U levels, along the lines of the discussion in Chapter IV.

Pending changes in world policy and action for accelerated economic growth, the present outlook is for the significantly reduced rates of demand growth for raw

---

[12]The aluminum exception must be kept in mind (see above, pp. 54-57).

materials, i.e., rates of the order of those for 1975-1985 and 1975-2000 shown in Tables 5-2.1 to 5-2.12. This obviously means growth reductions of approximately the same amount in the materials the world will need to supply. Presented here is an illustrative calculation for a few raw materials that makes this last point with particular reference to demand and supply for the non-U.S. world. Tables 5c and 5d (pages 95-96) examine the rate of growth of supply (column 6 in both Tables) needed to meet non-U.S. world demand, 1951-75 and 1975-2000. Essentially the required growth rates of supply for the five materials shown can be reduced by 50% or more in order to meet the total non-U.S. world demand—after U.S. needs are met. In the future, there may be significantly reduced pressures than have recently prevailed for expansion of output of key industrial raw materials in the world.

This probably means a period when market pressures will tend toward easing of relative prices for these materials. It is in general not the situation of a world confronted with materials exhaustion and that type of threat to economic expansion. Present understanding of the fundamental nature of the economic growth process encourages the expectation that sooner or later man and his public and private institutions will take actions toward altering the present prospect for limited GDP growth. Sooner or later this hopeful prospect will offset the force of one of the factors that contributes to this relative ease in the world materials outlook. More rapid GDP growth can in turn be expected to generate further declines in the I-U of raw materials.

The long-term views embody the basic nature of the intensity-of-use phenomenon. Man's knowledge and man's aspirations will achieve continuation of the I-U patterns discussed here. These quality-of-human inputs, not the quantity-of-material inputs, also assure that GDP per capita can expect to reach levels consistent with the desires and capabilities of man and of his national and international institutions.

Table 5-1.1
World Demand for Crude Steel
(million metric tons)
5-year averages

Region	1951-55	1961-65	1971-75	1985	2000*	
1. W. Europe	49.575	114.254	145.862	190.0	267.0	(361.0)
2. Japan	6.245	34.821	70.851	112.0	179.0	(203.0)
3. ODL	9.342	16.747	27.289	38.0	54.0	(61.0)
4. U.S.S.R.	34.253	77.494	128.917	182.0	263.0	(319.0)
5. E. Europe	22.971	33.212	45.936	68.0	99.0	(104.0)
6. Africa	1.290	2.492	4.898	8.0	15.0	(16.0)
7. Asia	3.516	12.225	29.255	45.0	72.0	(68.0)
8. L. America	5.096	13.691	24.961	41.0	72.0	(68.0)
9. China	2.233	12.164	29.017	44.0	67.0	(86.0)
10. U.S.	91.092	105.845	135.322	168.0	213.0	(266.0)
Totals						
11. World	225.613	422.945	642.308	896.0	1301.0	(1552.0)
12. Non-U.S. World	134.521	317.100	506.986	728.0	1088.0	(1286.0)
13. Poor Nations	12.135	40.572	88.131	139.0	226.0	(238.0)
14. Rich Nations	213.478	382.372	554.177	758.0	1075.0	(1314.0)

Source: Appendix Table V-1. The figures for 1985 and 2000 are the products of corresponding regional entries for 1985 and 2000 in Tables 3-2.1 and 4-1.

* Bracketed figures from *NCMP, 1973*.

Table 5-1.2
World Demand for Iron Ore
(million metric tons of iron content)
5-year averages

Region	1951-55	1961-65	1971-75	1985	2000*	
1. W. Europe	40.623	76.761	94.512	133.0	189.0	(232.0)
2. Japan	2.943	26.969	52.761	78.0	129.0	(161.0)
3. ODL	5.941	15.812	24.312	35.0	49.0	(49.0)
4. U.S.S.R.	28.761	65.885	96.921	144.0	209.0	(235.0)
5. E. Europe	6.212	16.574	26.275	36.0	50.0	(58.0)
6. Africa	1.214	2.291	3.779	8.0	14.0	(9.0)
7. Asia	2.146	5.541	10.004	18.0	33.0	(41.0)
8. L. America	1.522	7.577	14.698	25.0	48.0	(50.0)
9. China	2.196	11.800	23.211	39.0	65.0	(110.0)
10. U.S.	59.572	71.871	85.423	106.0	133.0	(141.0)
Totals						
11. World	151.129	301.081	431.896	622.0	919.0	(1086.0)
12. Non-U.S. World	91.557	229.210	346.473	516.0	786.0	(945.0)
13. Poor Nations	7.078	27.209	51.692	90.0	160.0	(210.0)
14. Rich Nations	144.051	273.872	380.204	532.0	759.0	(834.0)

Source: Appendix Table V-2. The figures for 1985 and 2000 are the products of corresponding regional entries for 1985 and 2000 in Tables 3-2.1 and 4-2.

* Bracketed figures from *NCMP (1973)*.

Table 5-1.3
World Demand for Nickel
(1000 metric tons)
5-year averages

Region	1951-55	1961-65	1971-75	1985	2000
1. W. Europe	52.7	101.3	169.6	245.9	345.0
2. Japan	4.4	23.6	97.3	155.2	245.3
3. ODL*	3.3	7.6	16.7	23.7	34.3
4. U.S.S.R., E. Europe & China	NA	105.2	159.4	241.5	360.2
6. Africa*	0.1	0.9	4.4	7.5	11.1
7. Asia	0.3	1.6	3.7	7.6	14.3
8. L. America	0.4	1.2	6.7	12.6	23.8
10. U.S.	69.3	122.1	160.5	210.5	280.1
Totals					
11. World	NA	363.4	618.4	904.5	1314.1
12. Non-U.S. World	NA	241.3	457.8	694.0	1034.0

Source: Appendix Table V-3. The figures for 1985 and 2000 are the products of corresponding regional entries for 1985 and 2000 in Tables 3-2.1 and 4-3.

* South Africa included with Africa (line 6).

Table 5-1.4
World Demand for Manganese Ore
(1000 metric tons)
5-year averages

Region	1951-55	1961-65	1971-75*	1985	2000
1. W. Europe	1647	2664	4134	5620	8348
2. Japan	336	758	1667	2586	4285
3. ODL	421	619	789	1168	1743
4. U.S.S.R.	3297	5786	6420	9500	14696
5. E. Europe	705	1096	1157	1785	2778
6. Africa	99	221	481	820	1513
7. Asia	180	669	1384	2265	3824
8. L. America	180	673	1071	1890	3703
9. China	170	919	998	1658	3168
10. U.S.	1768	1909	1929	2189	2668
Totals					
11. World	8803	15314	20030	29481	46726
12. Non-U.S. World	7035	13405	18101	27292	44058
13. Poor Nations	629	2483	3934	6633	12208
14. Rich Nations	8174	12831	16096	22848	34518

Source: Appendix Table V-4. The figures for 1985 and 2000 are the products of corresponding regional entries for 1985 and 2000 in Tables 3-2.1 and 4-4.

* Preliminary. In particular the ODL figure (3) is uncertain due to inventory adjustments.

Table 5-1.5
World Demand for Chrome Ore
(1000 metric tons)
5-year averages

Region	1951-55	1961-65	1971-75*	1985	2000
1. W. Europe	719	1080	1873	2951	4452
2. Japan	76	365	1127	1836	3233
3. ODL	233	256	740	1140	1877
4. U.S.S.R.	320	485	750	864	1083
5. E. Europe	181	352	744	1249	2047
6. Africa	9	18	49	82	142
7. Asia	30	52	184	302	526
8. L. America	12	21	109	221	423
9. China	14	58	216	375	634
10. U.S.	1131	1188	1149	1238	1334
Totals					
11. World	2725	3875	6941	10258	15751
12. Non-U.S. World	1594	2687	5792	9020	14417
13. Poor Nations	65	149	558	980	1725
14. Rich Nations	2660	3726	6383	9278	14026

Source: Appendix Table V-5. The figures for 1985 and 2000 are the products of corresponding regional entries for 1985 and 2000 in Tables 3-2.1 and 4-5.

*Preliminary.

Table 5-1.6
World Demand for Cobalt
(metric tons)
5-year averages

Region	1951-55	1961-65	1971-75*	1985	2000
1. W. Europe	2490	4780	6113	8711	12465
2. Japan	261	1487	3941	6379	10750
3. ODL	491	1069	1506	2224	3397
4. U.S.S.R.	463	932	1981	3040	4641
5. E. Europe	435	885	1108	1785	2750
6. Africa	345	520	706	1144	1958
7. Asia	9	68	255	846	1721
8. L. America	88	96	342	882	1904
9. China	16	46	200	442	1126
10. U.S.	4407	5046	7282	10778	16008
Totals					
11. World	8965	14929	23434	36231	56720
12. Non-U.S. World	4558	9883	16152	25453	40712
13. Poor Nations	458	730	1503	3314	6709
14. Rich Nations	8507	14199	21932	32917	50011

Source: Appendix Table V-6. The figures for 1985 and 2000 are the products of corresponding regional entries for 1985 and 2000 in Tables 3-2.1 and 4-6.

* Preliminary.

Table 5-1.7
World Demand for Tungsten
(metric tons)
5-year averages

Region	1951-55	1961-65	1971-75*	1985	2000
1. W. Europe	5170	8456	11575	16860	24486
2. Japan	496	1970	2758	4310	7011
3. ODL	101	342	578	834	1252
4. U.S.S.R.	3581	5442	6645	9975	14697
5. E. Europe	1090	2160	3824	6069	3669
6. Africa	61	72	685	1090	1807
7. Asia	430	534	849	1510	2868
8. L. America	562	281	1372	2520	4761
9. China	2320	3649	5386	8619	14080
10. U.S.	3699	5630	6510	8420	12006
Totals					
11. World	17510	28536	40182	60207	92637
12. Non-U.S. World	13811	22906	33672	51787	80631
13. Poor Nations	3373	4536	8292	13789	23516
14. Rich Nations	14137	24000	31890	46419	69121

Source: Appendix Table V-7. The figures for 1985 and 2000 are the products of corresponding regional entries for 1985 and 2000 in Tables 3-2.1 and 4-7.

* Preliminary.

Table 5-1.8
World Demand for Refined Copper
(1000 metric tons)
5-year averages

Region	1951-55	1961-65	1971-75	1985	2000*	
1. W. Europe	1142.94	1919.38	2421.72	3442.0	5231.0	(5354.0)
2. Japan	98.30	382.20	921.96	1358.0	2181.0	(2996.0)
3. ODL	168.34	333.78	356.62	528.0	715.0	(1078.0)
4. U.S.S.R.	386.00	728.18	1097.00	1440.0	2088.0	(2940.0)
5. E. Europe	146.66	282.82	539.20	785.0	1199.0	(920.0)
6. Africa	5.70	11.54	20.80	38.0	71.0	(111.0)
7. Asia	34.78	97.42	110.88	181.0	311.0	(476.0)
8. L. America	78.58	125.26	278.08	473.0	873.0	(589.0)
9. China	7.60	110.00	290.00	486.0	968.0	(840.0)
10. U.S.	1298.12	1681.26	1886.08	2610.0	3202.0	(4389.0)
Totals						
11. World	3367.02	5671.84	7922.71	11341.0	16839.0	(19693.0)
12. Non-U.S. World	2068.90	3990.58	6036.62	8731.0	13637.0	(15304.0)
13. Poor Nations	126.66	344.22	699.77	1178.0	2223.0	(2016.0)
14. Rich Nations	3240.36	5327.62	7222.94	10163.0	14616.0	(17677.0)

Source: Appendix Table V-8. The figures for 1985 and 2000 are the products of corresponding regional entries for 1985 and 2000 in Tables 3-2.1 and 4-8.

* Bracketed figures from *NCMP 1973*.

Table 5-1.9
World Demand for Primary Aluminum
(1000 metric tons)
5-year averages

Region	1951-55	1965-65	1971-75	1985	2000*	
1. W. Europe	608.96	1380.98	2861.62	4637.0	7791.0	(10320.0)
2. Japan	38.04	227.80	1253.66	2414.0	4674.0	(6420.0)
3. ODL	93.62	200.40	527.70	890.0	1565.0	(2009.0)
4. U.S.S.R.	286.00	804.60	1490.00	2352.0	3868.0	(6552.0)
5. E. Europe	75.68	316.40	826.62	1339.0	2457.0	(2358.0)
6. Africa	0.96	7.06	39.92	65.0	160.0	(167.0)
7. Asia	10.80	91.62	294.34	453.0	884.0	(1088.0)
8. L. America	24.66	98.22	332.72	599.0	1217.0	(1116.0)
9. China	2.70	86.80	234.00	431.0	827.0	(1056.0)
10. U.S.	1211.25	2321.48	4388.10	7410.0	13073.0	(15657.0)
Totals						
11. World	2351.77	5535.36	12248.69	20590.0	36516.0	(46761.0)
12. Non-U.S. World	1140.42	3213.88	7860.59	13180.0	23443.0	(31104.0)
13. Poor Nations	39.12	283.70	900.98	1548.0	3088.0	(3427.0)
14. Rich Nations	2312.56	5251.66	11347.71	19042.0	33428.0	(43334.0)

Source: Appendix Table V-9. The figures for 1985 and 2000 are the products of corresponding regional entries for 1985 and 2000 in Tables 3-2.1 and 4-9.

* Bracketed figures from *NCMP 1973*.

Table 5-1.10
World Demand for the Platinum-Group
(1000 troy ounces)
5-year averages

Region	1951-55	1961-65	1971-75*	1985	2000
1. W. Europe	151.1	408.9	653.2	948.0	1391.0
2. Japan	18.0	317.9	1765.1	3146.0	5765.0
3. ODL†	36.3	158.2	271.7	403.0	625.0
4. U.S.S.R. and					
E. Europe	NA	304.6	701.7	1218.0	1806.0
6. Africa	0.3	4.1	38.2	65.0	129.0
7. Asia	4.7	20.4	140.7	242.0	418.0
8. L. America	12.7	18.4	34.0	79.0	158.0
9. China†	NA	8.0	123.0	210.0	343.0
10. U.S.	576.6	999.5	1659.6	2442.0	3335.0
Totals					
11. World	NA	2240.0	5387.2	8753.0	14030.0
12. Non-U.S. World	NA	1240.5	3727.6	6311.0	10695.0
13. Poor Nations	NA	50.9	335.9	596.0	1048.0
14. Rich Nations	NA	2189.1	5051.3	8157.0	12982.0

Source: Appendix Table V-10. The figures for 1985 and 2000 are the products of corresponding regional entries for 1985 and 2000 in Tables 3-2.1 and 4-10.

*Preliminary. In particular regions (4)-(9) based on 1971-73 approximations.

†Approximate.

Table 5-1.11
World Demand for Zinc
(1000 metric tons)
5-year averages

Region	1951-55	1961-65	1971-75	1985	2000*	
1. W. Europe	742.82	1173.98	1555.01	2178.0	3116.0	(3483.0)
2. Japan	83.50	295.12	673.42	1034.0	1441.0	(1846.0)
3. ODL	121.68	201.78	316.40	459.0	704.0	(772.0)
4. U.S.S.R.	232.86	386.08	832.12	1296.0	1934.0	(1470.0)
5. E. Europe	120.14	260.50	452.30	625.0	965.0	(1006.0)
6. Africa	0.60	5.28	24.48	38.0	71.0	(46.0)
7. Asia	28.20	114.66	207.73	347.0	574.0	(663.0)
8. L. America	46.70	96.80	226.02	378.0	688.0	(620.0)
9. China	5.80	94.04	190.01	298.0	528.0	(720.0)
10. U.S.	863.26	1014.66	1159.82	1600.0	2001.0	(2822.0)
Totals						
11. World	2240.34	3558.26	5506.26	8253.0	12022.0	(13448.0)
12. Non-U.S. World	1377.08	2543.60	4346.21	6653.0	10021.0	(10626.0)
13. Poor Nations	76.08	226.14	649.10	1061.0	1861.0	(2049.0)
14. Rich Nations	2164.26	3332.12	4989.93	7192.0	10161.0	(11399.0)

Source: Appendix Table V-11. The figures for 1985 and 2000 are the products of corresponding regional entries for 1985 and 2000 in Tables 3-2.1 and 4-11.

* Bracketed figures from *NCMP 1973*.

81

Table 5-1.12
World Demand for Tin
(1000 metric tons)
5-year averages

Region	1951-55	1961-65	1971-75	1985	2000
1. W. Europe	54.30	67.94	68.84	84.0	111.0
2. Japan	5.62	16.08	32.76	47.0	62.0
3. ODL	8.26	10.90	11.82	15.0	22.0
4. U.S.S.R.	12.96	25.70	18.40	24.0	31.0
5. E. Europe	6.10	9.24	17.14	23.0	32.0
6. Africa	1.22	1.68	1.78	7.0†	10.0†
7. Asia	4.68	6.34	7.62	11.0	14.0
8. L. America	4.62	6.02	7.32	11.0	16.0
9. China	2.08	13.10	14.48	20.0	28.0
10. U.S.	55.98	56.22	52.56	59.0	67.0
Totals					
11. World	155.82	213.22	232.72	301.0	393.0
12. Non-U.S. World	99.84	157.00	180.16	242.0	326.0
13. Poor Nations	12.60	27.14	31.20	49.0	68.0
14. Rich Nations	143.22	186.08	201.52	252.0	325.0

Source: Appendix Table V-12. The figures for 1985 and 2000 are the products of corresponding regional entries for 1985 and 2000 in Tables 3-2.1 and 4-12.

†Tentative.

Table 5-2.1

World Demand for Crude Steel: Annual Rates of Growth*

Region	1951-75	1975-85	1975 -	2000**
1. W. Europe	5.5	2.1	2.2	(3.4)
2. Japan	12.9	3.7	3.4	(4.4)
3. ODL	5.5	2.7	2.5	(3.4)
4. U.S.S.R.	6.9	2.8	2.6	(3.6)
5. E. Europe	3.5	3.2	2.8	(3.4)
6. Africa	6.9	4.0	4.2	(5.6)
7. Asia	11.2	3.5	3.3	(5.4)
8. L. America	8.3	4.0	3.9	(5.1)
9. China	13.7	3.4	3.1	(5.3)
10. U.S.	2.0	1.7	1.7	(2.1)
Totals				
11. World	5.4	2.7	2.6	(3.5)
12. Non-U.S. World	6.9	2.9	2.8	(3.6)
13. Poor Nations	10.4	3.7	3.5	(5.3)
14. Rich Nations	4.9	2.5	2.4	(3.0)

*Annual rates based on 5-year periods: thus 1951-75 refers to 20-year period from 1951-55 to 1971-75.

1975-85 refers to 12.5-year period from 1971-75 to a 5-year period centered at 1985.

1975-2000 refers to 27.5-year period from 1971-75 to a 5-year period centered at 2000.

**Bracketed rates are comparable magnitudes estimated in an earlier study, *NCMP 1973* (see text).

Table 5-2.2
World Demand for Iron Ore: Annual Rates of Growth*

Region	1951-75	1975-85	1975 -	2000**
1. W. Europe	4.4	2.8	2.6	(3.1)
2. Japan	16.0	3.2	3.3	(4.3)
3. ODL	7.5	3.0	2.6	(3.2)
4. U.S.S.R.	6.4	3.2	2.8	(3.6)
5. E. Europe	7.7	2.4	2.3	(3.3)
6. Africa	6.0	6.2	4.8	(5.4)
7. Asia	8.2	4.8	4.4	(5.5)
8. L. America	12.3	4.3	4.4	(5.2)
9. China	13.0	4.2	3.8	(5.0)
10. U.S.	1.8	1.7	1.6	(2.0)
Totals				
11. World	5.5	3.0	2.8	(3.5)
12. Non-U.S. World	7.1	3.2	3.0	(3.8)
13. Poor Nations	10.7	4.5	4.2	(5.1)
14. Rich Nations	5.1	2.7	2.5	(3.1)

*As in Table 5-2.1   **As in Table 5-2.1.

Table 5-2.3

World Demand for Nickel: Annual Rates of Growth*

Region	1951-75	1975-85	1975-2000
1. W. Europe	6.0	3.0	2.6
2. Japan	16.7	3.8	3.4
3. ODL	8.5	2.8	2.7
4. U.S.S.R., China &			
E. Europe	7.0†	3.4	3.0
6. Africa	19.8	4.3	3.4
7. Asia	13.1	6.0	5.1
8. L. America	15.8	5.1	4.7
10. U.S.	4.3	2.2	2.0
Totals			
11. World	6.5†	3.1	2.8
12. Non-U.S. World	8.2†	3.4	3.0

*As in Table 5-2.1.   †1956-75.

Table 5-2.4

World Demand for Manganese Ore: Annual Rates of Growth*

Region	1951-75	1975-85	1975-2000
1. W. Europe	4.7	2.4	2.6
2. Japan	8.3	3.6	3.5
3. ODL	4.9	3.2	2.9
4. U.S.S.R.	3.5	3.2	3.1
5. E. Europe	2.6	3.5	3.2
6. Africa	8.2	4.4	4.3
7. Asia	10.7	4.0	3.8
8. L. America	9.3	4.6	4.6
9. China	9.3	4.1	4.3
10. U.S.	0.4	1.0	1.2
Totals			
11. World	4.2	3.1	3.1
12. Non-U.S. World	4.8	3.3	3.3
13. Poor Nations	9.6	4.3	4.2
14. Rich Nations	3.5	2.8	2.8

*As in Table 5-2.1

Table 5-2.5

World Demand for Chrome Ore: Annual Rates of Growth*

Region	1951-75	1975-85	1975-2000
1. W. Europe	4.9	3.7	3.2
2. Japan	14.4	4.0	3.9
3. ODL	5.9	3.5	3.4
4. U.S.S.R.	4.4	1.1	1.3
5. E. Europe	7.3	4.2	3.7
6. Africa	8.8	4.2	3.9
7. Asia	9.5	4.0	3.9
8. L. America	11.6	5.8	5.1
9. China	14.6	4.5	4.9
10. U.S.	0.1	0.6	0.5
Totals			
11. World	4.8	3.2	3.0
12. Non-U.S. World	6.7	3.6	3.4
13. Poor Nations	11.3	4.6	4.2
14. Rich Nations	4.5	3.0	2.9

*As in Table 5-2.1.

Table 5-2.6
World Demand for Cobalt: Annual Rates of Growth*

Region	1951-75	1975-85	1975-2000
1. W. Europe	4.6	2.9	2.6
2. Japan	14.5	3.9	3.7
3. ODL	5.8	3.2	3.0
4. U.S.S.R.	8.0	3.5	3.1
5. E. Europe	4.8	3.9	3.4
6. Africa	3.6	3.9	3.8
7. Asia	18.2	10.1	7.2
8. L. America	7.0	7.9	6.4
9. China	13.5	6.5	6.5
10. U.S.	2.5	3.2	2.9
Totals			
11. World	4.9	3.5	3.3
12. Non-U.S. World	6.5	3.7	3.4
13. Poor Nations	6.1	6.5	5.6
14. Rich Nations	4.8	3.3	3.0

*As in Table 5-2.1.

Table 5-2.7
World Demand for Tungsten: Annual Rates of Growth*

Region	1951-75	1975-85	1975-2000
1. W. Europe	4.1	3.1	2.8
2. Japan	9.0	3.6	3.5
3. ODL	9.1	3.0	2.9
4. U.S.S.R.	3.1	3.3	2.9
5. E. Europe	6.5	3.8	3.4
6. Africa	12.8	3.8	3.6
7. Asia	3.5	4.7	4.5
8. L. America	4.6	5.0	4.6
9. China	4.3	3.8	3.0
10. U.S.	2.9	2.1	2.3
Totals			
11. World	4.2	3.3	3.1
12. Non-U.S. World	4.6	3.5	3.2
13. Poor Nations	4.6	4.2	3.9
14. Rich Nations	4.1	3.0	2.9

* As in Table 5-2.1.

Table 5-2.8
World Demand for Refined Copper: Annual Rates of Growth*

Region	1951-75	1975-85	1975 -	2000**
1. W. Europe	3.8	2.9	2.8	(3.0)
2. Japan	12.0	3.1	3.2	(4.8)
3. ODL	3.8	3.2	2.6	(3.4)
4. U.S.S.R.	5.4	2.2	2.4	(3.8)
5. E. Europe	6.7	3.1	3.0	(3.4)
6. Africa	6.7	4.9	4.6	(7.1)
7. Asia	6.0	4.0	3.8	(4.4)
8. L. America	6.5	4.3	4.2	(4.9)
9. China	20.0	4.8	4.5	(5.4)
10. U.S.	1.9	2.6	1.9	(2.6)
Totals				
11. World	4.4	2.9	2.8	(3.4)
12. Non-U.S. World	5.5	3.0	3.0	(3.7)
13. Poor Nations	8.9	4.3	4.3	(5.3)
14. Rich Nations	4.1	2.8	2.6	(3.3)

*As in Table 5-2.1.   **As in Table 5-2.1.

Table 5-2.9

World Demand for Primary Aluminum: Annual Rates of Growth*

Region	1951-75	1975-85	1975 -	2000**
1. W. Europe	8.0	3.9	3.7	(5.2)
2. Japan	19.1	5.4	4.9	(7.6)
3. ODL	9.0	4.3	4.0	(5.8)
4. U.S.S.R.	8.6	3.7	3.5	(5.4)
5. E. Europe	12.7	3.9	4.0	(4.8)
6. Africa	20.5	4.0	5.2	(7.1)
7. Asia	18.0	4.0	4.1	(5.7)
8. L. America	13.9	4.8	4.8	(6.3)
9. China	25.0	5.0	4.7	(6.6)
10. U.S.	6.6	4.3	4.0	(4.8)
Totals				
11. World	8.6	4.2	4.1	(5.4)
12. Non-U.S. World	10.1	4.2	4.1	(5.7)
13. Poor Nations	17.0	4.4	4.6	(6.2)
14. Rich Nations	8.3	4.2	4.0	(5.3)

*As in Table 5-2.1.   **As in Table 5-2.1.

Table 5-2.10

World Demand for the Platinum-Group: Annual Rates of Growth*

Region	1951-75	1975-85	1975-2000
1. W. Europe	7.6	3.0	2.8
2. Japan	25.8	4.7	3.6
3. ODL	10.6	3.2	3.1
4. U.S.S.R. & E. Europe	NA	4.5	3.6
6. Africa	27.4	4.3	4.5
7. Asia	18.5	4.4	4.0
8. L. America	5.0	4.4	5.7
9. China	NA	4.3	3.8
10. U.S.	5.4	3.1	2.6
Totals			
11. World	9.2**	4.0	3.5
12. Non-U.S. World	11.6**	4.3	3.9
13. Poor Nations	20.8**	4.7	4.2
14. Rich Nations	8.7**	3.9	3.5

* As in Table 5-2.1.

** Refers to 1961-75 period.

Table 5-2.11
World Demand for Zinc: Annual Rates of Growth*

Region	1951-75	1975-85	1975 -	2000**
1. W. Europe	3.8	2.7	2.6	(3.0)
2. Japan	11.0	3.5	2.8	(4.1)
3. ODL	4.9	3.0	3.0	(3.4)
4. U.S.S.R.	6.6	3.6	3.1	(3.6)
5. E. Europe	6.9	2.6	2.8	(3.3)
6. Africa	20.4	3.6	3.9	(5.9)
7. Asia	11.0	4.2	3.8	(4.6)
8. L. America	8.2	4.2	4.1	(4.8)
9. China	19.1	3.7	3.8	(5.3)
10. U.S.	1.5	2.6	2.0	(2.6)
Totals				
11. World	4.6	3.3	2.9	(3.4)
12. Non-U.S. World	5.9	3.5	3.1	(3.6)
13. Poor Nations	11.3	4.0	3.9	(5.0)
14. Rich Nations	4.3	3.0	2.6	(3.2)

*As in Table 5-2.1.   **As in Table 5-2.1.

Table 5-2.12
World Demand for Tin: Annual Rates of Growth *

Region	1951-75	1975-85	1975-2000
1. W. Europe	1.2	1.6	1.8
2. Japan	9.2	2.9	2.3
3. ODL	1.8	1.9	2.3
4. U.S.S.R.	1.8	2.1	1.9
5. E. Europe	5.3	2.4	2.3
6. Africa	1.9	11.6 †	6.5 †
7. Asia	2.4	3.0	2.2
8. L. America	2.3	3.3	2.9
9. China	10.2	2.6	2.4
10. U.S.	−0.4	0.9	0.9
Totals			
11. World	2.0	2.1	1.9
12. Non-U.S. World	3.0	2.4	2.2
13. Poor Nations	4.6	3.7 †	2.9 †
14. Rich Nations	1.7	1.8	1.8

* As in Table 5-2.1.   †Tentative projections; 1971-75 base for Africa may need revision.

Table 5c

Production Implications of Foreign Materials Requirements in 2000
Historical

Metal	U.S. Demand (1)	U.S. Production (2)	U.S. Gap (3)	Non-U.S. World Demand (4)	Non-U.S. Demand plus U.S. Gap (5)	Rate of Growth (6)
Iron Ore (m.m.t)						
1951-55 (avg.)	59.57	52.84	6.73	91.55	98.28	7.0%
1971-75 (avg.)	85.42	49.75*	35.67	346.47	382.14	
Aluminum (t.m.t)						
1951-55 (avg.)	1211.25	1098.16	113.09	1140.42	1253.51	10.0%
1971-75 (avg.)	4388.10	3875.36	512.74	7860.59	8373.33	
Zinc (t.m.t)						
1951-55 (avg.)	863.26	864.30	−1.04	1377.08	1376.04	6.6%
1971-75 (avg.)	1159.82	607.92	551.90	4346.21	4898.11	
Copper (t.m.t)						
1951-55 (avg.)	1298.12	1308.32	−10.20	2068.90	2058.70	5.5%
1971-75 (avg.)	1886.08	1895.32	9.24	6036.62	6045.86	
Platinum-Group (t.tr oz)						
1951-55 (avg.)	576.56	28.96	547.60	325.00*	872.60	9.5%
1971-75 (avg.)	1659.62	16.94*	1642.68	3727.52	5370.20	

Source: Appendix Tables V.2, V.8 to V.11. U.S.B.M. *Minerals Yearbook* (annual). Metallgesellschaft Aktiengesellschaft. *Metal Statistics* (annual)

*Preliminary

Table 5d

Production Implications of Foreign Materials Requirements in 2000 Projected

Metal	U.S. Demand (1)	U.S. Production (2)	U.S. Gap (3)	Non-U.S. World Demand (4)	Non-U.S. Demand plus U.S. Gap (5)	Rate of Growth (6)
Iron Ore (m.m.t)						
2000	133.0	55.0*	78.0	786.0	864.0	3.0%
Aluminum (t.m.t)						
2000	13073.0	12000.0*	1073.0	23443.0	24516.0	4.0%
Zinc (t.m.t)						
2000	2001.0	535.0*	1466.0	10021.0	11487.0	3.1%
Copper (t.m.t)						
2000	3202.0	2800.0†	402.0	13637.0	14039.0	3.1%
Platinum-Group (t.tr oz)						
2000	3335.0	28.0†	3307.0	10695.0	14002.0	3.5%

Sources: Tables 5-1.2, 5-1.8-11: U.S.B.M., *Mineral Facts and Problems*, (1976): N.C.M.P., *Materials Requirements in the U.S. and Abroad in the Year 2000* (1973)

*National Commission on Materials Policy estimates (1973).

†Projection of primary production (U.S.B.M., *Mineral Facts and Problems*, 1976).

APPENDIX
Historical Data, Source Materials

Appendix Table III-1
GDP
Historical Data
Five-Year Averages (billions of U.S. dollars, 1971 prices)
Annual Rates of Growth (%)

	1934-38		1951-55		1956-60		1961-65		1966-70		1971-75	
	Average	%	Average	%	Average	%	Average	%	Average	%	Average	%
1. W. Europe	227.325	2.7	389.135	4.8	482.394	4.1	604.898	5.0	767.979	4.8	936.312	2.5
2. Japan	36.451	3.2	43.905	6.9	64.225	8.5	100.877	10.0	171.141	11.8	257.782	5.2
3. ODL	36.124	3.3	72.749	4.2	87.462	3.5	111.122	5.8	144.963	5.2	183.470	3.6
4. U.S.S.R.	116.936	5.6	209.847	7.1	292.390	6.4	382.040	5.3	495.827	5.5	617.416	4.0
5. E. Europe	NA	NA	86.411	5.9	113.412	5.4	140.827	3.8	174.595	4.7	226.676	6.1
6. Africa	NA	NA	26.172	5.9	35.038	5.6	43.271	4.6	55.639	5.5	71.391	4.6
7. Asia	NA	NA	76.916	3.9	96.005	4.3	119.918	4.7	154.807	6.0	201.457	4.7
8. L. America	NA	NA	66.846	5.3	86.539	5.3	111.706	5.2	147.361	6.0	200.275	6.0
9. China	NA	NA	62.000	9.5	87.200	4.3	84.000	1.7	107.400	4.7	143.604	5.7
10. U.S.	213.396	1.4	557.108	3.8	640.160	2.2	773.222	4.9	942.317	3.5	1122.094	2.2
Totals												
11. World	NA	NA	1591.088	5.0	1983.724	4.1	2471.881	5.0	3162.029	5.0	3960.477	3.5
12. Non-U.S. World	NA	NA	1033.981	5.7	1343.565	5.0	1698.659	5.0	2219.712	5.6	2838.383	4.4
13. Poor Nations	NA	NA	231.934	6.2	304.782	4.7	359.895	4.1	465.208	5.6	616.727	5.3
14. Rich Nations	NA	NA	1359.155	4.8	1680.043	4.0	2112.987	5.2	2696.821	3.9	3343.750	3.2

Source: United Nations. *Statistical Yearbook* (annual); U.N. *Yearbook of National Account Statistics* (annual); International Bank for Reconstruction and Development. *World Bank Atlas*, 1977. also see text, Chapter III

Appendix Table III-2
Population
Historical Data

Five-Year Averages (millions of people)
Annual Rates of Growth (%)

	1934-38 Average	%	1951-55 Average	%	1956-60 Average	%	1961-65 Average	%	1966-70 Average	%	1971-75 Average	%
1. W. Europe	284.840	0.5	314.100	0.8	328.200	0.9	345.900	1.1	364.100	1.0	379.280	0.7
2. Japan	69.400	0.8	86.500	1.3	91.320	0.9	96.040	1.1	101.300	1.1	107.580	1.3
3. ODL	30.260	1.2	40.660	2.6	46.260	2.6	51.820	2.1	57.460	2.1	63.940	2.0
4. U.S.S.R.	162.160	0.9	189.400	1.7	206.700	1.8	224.000	1.5	237.600	1.0	250.040	1.0
5. E. Europe	97.940	0.9	109.600	1.1	114.800	0.9	119.600	0.8	124.700	0.9	129.780	0.7
6. Africa	NA	NA	218.000	2.1	242.600	2.2	271.300	2.3	308.300	2.7	353.580	2.7
7. Asia	NA	NA	726.200	1.9	810.000	2.3	911.800	2.4	1042.000	2.8	1199.380	2.6
8. L. America	NA	NA	170.000	2.7	194.700	2.8	223.600	2.8	259.000	3.0	298.660	2.8
9. China	NA	NA	594.000	1.7	650.100	1.9	712.600	1.9	781.200	1.8	852.460	1.7
10. U.S.	128.040	0.5	160.200	1.7	174.400	1.7	189.000	1.5	201.100	1.1	213.740	0.9
Totals												
11. World	NA	NA	2609.000	1.8	2859.000	1.9	3146.000	1.9	3477.000	2.0	3848.200	1.9
12. Non-U.S. World	NA	NA	2448.000	1.8	2685.000	1.9	2957.000	2.0	3276.000	2.1	3634.500	1.9
13. Poor Nations	NA	NA	1708.000	2.0	1897.000	2.2	2119.000	2.3	2390.000	2.5	2703.400	2.4
14. Rich Nations	772.640	0.7	900.500	1.3	961.700	1.3	1026.000	1.3	1086.000	1.1	1144.200	1.0

Source   United Nations. *Demographic Yearbook* (various issues 1948-1974): U.N. *Population by Sex and Age for Regions and Countries, 1950-2000 as Assessed in 1973 Medium Variant* (1976); U.N. *World Population Prospects as Assessed in 1968* (1973)

Appendix Table III-3
GDP per Capita
Historical Data

Five-Year Averages (U.S. dollars, 1971 prices)
Annual Rates of Growth (%)

	1934-38 Average	%	1951-55 Average	%	1956-60 Average	%	1961-65 Average	%	1966-70 Average	%	1971-75 Average	%
1. W. Europe	955.733	2.7	1238.040	4.0	1468.970	3.2	1747.230	3.8	2107.870	3.8	2468.650	1.8
2. Japan	524.834	2.9	506.825	5.4	702.377	7.5	1048.560	8.9	1685.770	10.5	2388.880	3.9
3. ODL	1192.940	1.3	1787.750	1.5	1889.820	0.8	2141.210	3.6	2519.720	3.1	2869.409	1.6
4. U.S.S.R.	720.122	5.8	1105.800	5.3	1412.170	4.5	1703.370	3.7	2085.000	4.4	2469.270	3.0
5. E. Europe	NA	NA	787.929	4.8	986.922	4.5	1176.530	3.0	1399.270	3.8	1746.617	5.4
6. Africa	NA	NA	119.900	2.7	139.669	3.3	159.323	2.2	180.202	2.7	201.909	1.9
7. Asia	NA	NA	105.796	2.9	118.418	1.9	131.384	2.2	148.376	3.1	167.967	2.1
8. L. America	NA	NA	392.687	2.5	443.840	2.4	498.988	2.3	567.957	2.9	670.578	3.2
9. China	NA	NA	104.149	7.7	134.050	2.4	117.650	−1.2	137.381	2.8	168.458	4.0
10. U.S.	1666.250	1.1	3474.320	2.1	3670.880	0.5	4086.680	3.3	4683.410	2.4	5249.808	1.3
Totals												
11. World	NA	NA	609.243	3.2	693.275	2.1	784.831	3.0	908.493	2.9	1029.180	1.6
12. Non-U.S. World	NA	NA	421.739	3.9	499.884	3.0	573.771	3.1	676.746	3.5	780.956	2.5
13. Poor Nations	NA	NA	135.570	4.2	159.889	2.5	169.116	1.8	194.359	3.0	228.130	2.9
14. Rich Nations	NA	NA	1507.940	3.5	1745.780	2.6	2056.500	3.9	2480.770	2.8	2922.397	2.2

Source: Appendix Tables III-1 and III-2.

Appendix Table IV-1
Intensity-of-Use: Crude Steel
(1000 metric tons per billion $ GDP)

Region	1934-38	1951-55	1956-60	1961-65	1966-70	1971-75
1. W. Europe	196.2	127.4	159.4	188.9	160.0	155.8
2. Japan	NA	142.2	294.5	345.2	303.7	274.6
3. ODL	NA	128.4	144.8	150.7	149.1	149.1
4. U.S.S.R.	127.2	163.2	187.9	202.8	204.0	208.9
5. E. Europe	NA	265.8	237.0	235.8	205.7	202.4
6. Africa	NA	49.3	55.2	57.6	56.1	68.9
7. Asia	NA	45.7	105.8	101.9	95.4	145.6
8. L. America	NA	76.2	109.6	122.6	103.8	124.8
9. China	NA	36.0	119.9	144.8	148.9	201.5
10. U.S.	177.9	163.5	141.0	136.9	140.6	120.6
Totals						
11. World	NA	141.8	157.5	171.1	162.9	162.2
12. Non-U.S. World	NA	130.1	165.4	186.7	172.4	178.6
13. Poor Nations	NA	52.3	105.3	113.0	105.7	142.8
14. Rich Nations	NA	157.1	167.0	181.0	172.8	165.7

Source: Appendix Tables III-1 and V-1.

Appendix Table IV-2
Intensity-of-Use: Iron Ore
(1000 metric tons per billion $ GDP)

Region	1934-38*	1951-55	1956-60	1961-65	1966-70	1971-75
1. W. Europe		104.4	123.8	126.9	112.1	101.0
2. Japan		67.0	209.7	267.3	239.5	204.5
3. ODL		81.7	113.9	142.3	127.7	132.9
4. U.S.S.R.		137.1	143.9	172.5	169.7	157.1
5. E. Europe		71.9	101.0	117.7	131.2	115.7
6. Africa		46.4	51.4	57.9	51.5	53.2
7. Asia		27.9	41.5	46.2	50.0	49.8
8. L. America		22.8	62.5	67.8	70.8	73.5
9. China		35.4	74.8	140.5	169.2	161.1
10. U.S.		106.9	106.9	92.9	81.9	76.1
Totals						
11. World		95.0	112.3	121.8	116.7	109.1
12. Non-U.S. World		88.5	114.9	134.9	131.5	122.1
13. Poor Nations		30.5	58.2	75.8	84.3	83.4
14. Rich Nations		106.0	122.1	129.6	122.3	113.7

Source: Appendix Tables III-1 and V-2.

*NA

Appendix Table IV-3
Intensity-of-Use: Nickel
(1000 metric tons per billion $ GDP)

Region	1934-38*	1951-55	1956-60	1961-65	1966-70	1971-75
1. W. Europe		135.4	137.2	167.5	188.6	181.1
2. Japan		100.7	152.9	233.6	373.8	377.4
3. ODL†		48.0	69.0	75.0	107.1	101.1
4. U.S.S.R., China & E. Europe		NA	117.3	173.3	153.0	161.4
6. Africa		3.9	6.0	16.0	54.1	49.4
7. Asia		4.0	4.4	13.2	11.1	18.2
8. L. America		5.4	7.9	10.6	13.2	33.7
10. U.S.		124.4	155.8	157.9	160.9	143.1
Totals						
11. World		NA	121.2	147.0	158.4	156.1
12. Non-U.S. World		NA	104.7	142.0	157.4	161.3

Source: Appendix Tables III-1 and V-3.

†South Africa included with Africa (line 6).

*NA

103

Appendix Table IV-4
Intensity-of-Use: Manganese Ore
(1000 metric tons per billion $ GDP)

Region	1934-38	1951-55	1956-60	1961-65	1966-70	1971-75
1. W. Europe	5.9	4.2	4.7	4.4	4.8	4.4
2. Japan	6.1	7.7	8.2	7.5	6.1	6.5
3. ODL	3.6	5.8	7.7	5.6	4.9	4.3
4. U.S.S.R.	14.8	15.7	15.2	15.2	11.6	10.4
5. E. Europe	NA	8.2	9.2	7.8	6.5	5.1
6. Africa	NA	3.8	4.8	4.9	5.5	6.7
7. Asia	NA	2.4	2.4	5.6	7.5	6.9
8. L. America	NA	2.7	2.1	6.0	4.7	5.4
9. China	NA	2.8	9.9	11.0	8.6	7.0
10. U.S.	2.9	3.2	2.7	2.5	2.2	1.7
Totals						
11. World	NA	5.5	6.1	6.2	5.5	5.1
12. Non-U.S. World	NA	6.8	7.7	7.9	4.7	6.5
13. Poor Nations	NA	2.7	4.8	6.9	6.6	6.4
14. Rich Nations	NA	6.0	6.4	6.1	5.4	4.8

Source: Appendix Tables III-1 and V-4.

Appendix Table IV-5
Intensity-of-Use: Chrome Ore
(metric tons per billion $ GDP)

Region	1934-38	1951-55	1956-60	1961-65	1966-70	1971-75
1. W. Europe	2019	1848	2042	1785	2475	2000
2. Japan	933	1731	3908	3619	4400	4372
3. ODL	997	3203	2390	2304	3435	4033
4. U.S.S.R.	1351	1525	1389	1270	1105	1215
5. E. Europe	NA	2095	2081	2500	2566	3282
6. Africa	NA	344	371	416	593	686
7. Asia	NA	390	427	434	601	913
8. L. America	NA	180	185	188	387	544
9. China	NA	226	275	690	1536	1504
10. U.S.	1818	2030	2093	1536	1337	1024
Totals						
11. World	NA	1713	1775	1568	1820	1753
12. Non-U.S. World	NA	1542	1623	1582	2025	2041
13. Poor Nations	NA	280	312	414	748	905
14. Rich Nations	NA	1957	2039	1763	2005	1909

Source: Appendix Tables III-1 and V-5.

Appendix Table IV-6
Intensity-of-Use: Cobalt
(metric tons per billion $ GDP)

Region	1934-38*	1951-55	1956-60	1961-65	1966-70	1971-75
1. W. Europe		6.4	5.2	9.5	7.6	6.5
2. Japan		5.9	12.2	14.7	19.8	15.3
3. ODL		6.7	10.7	9.6	8.1	8.2
4. U.S.S.R.		2.0	2.1	2.4	2.7	3.2
5. E. Europe		5.0	5.6	6.3	5.9	4.9
6. Africa		13.2	14.2	12.0	11.7	9.9
7. Asia		0.1	0.3	0.6	0.9	1.3
8. L. America		1.3	0.8	0.9	1.6	1.7
9. China		0.3	0.3	0.5	0.8	1.4
10. U.S.		7.9	6.4	6.5	6.8	6.5
Totals						
11. World		5.6	5.1	6.0	6.4	5.9
12. Non-U.S. World		4.4	4.5	5.8	6.2	5.7
13. Poor Nations		2.0	2.1	2.0	2.4	2.4
14. Rich Nations		6.3	5.7	6.7	7.1	6.6

Source: Appendix Tables III-1 and V-6.

*NA

Appendix Table IV-7
Intensity-of-Use: Tungsten
(metric tons per billion $ GDP)

Region	1934-38	1951-55	1956-60	1961-65	1966-70	1971-75
1. W. Europe	35.2	13.3	14.2	14.0	13.5	12.4
2. Japan	NA	11.3	17.4	19.5	16.4	10.7
3. ODL	2.2	1.4	1.6	3.1	6.1	3.2
4. U.S.S.R.	6.7	17.1	13.7	14.2	12.5	10.8
5. E. Europe	NA	12.7	14.2	15.3	19.9	16.9
6. Africa	NA	2.3	2.3	1.7	4.4	9.6
7. Asia	NA	5.6	5.8	4.5	5.8	4.2
8. L. America	NA	8.4	6.5	2.5	5.9	6.9
9. China	NA	37.4	34.7	43.4	44.7	37.5
10. U.S.	13.4	6.6	6.3	7.3	7.0	5.8
Totals						
11. World	NA	11.0	11.1	11.5	11.6	10.2
12. Non-U.S. World	NA	13.4	13.4	13.5	13.6	11.9
13. Poor Nations	NA	14.5	13.9	12.6	14.6	13.5
14. Rich Nations	NA	10.4	10.5	11.4	11.1	9.5

Source: Appendix Tables III-1 and V-7.

Appendix Table IV-8
Intensity-of-Use: Refined Copper
(metric tons per billion $ GDP)

Region	1934-38	1951-55	1956-60	1961-65	1966-70	1971-75
1. W. Europe	3307.0	2937.1	3315.1	3193.1	2675.9	2586.4
2. Japan	4116.0	2238.9	3067.3	3788.8	3998.1	3576.5
3. ODL	1591.0	2314.0	2209.2	3003.7	2529.3	1943.8
4. U.S.S.R.	1554.0	1839.4	1779.6	1906.0	1466.6	1776.8
5. E. Europe	NA	1697.2	1767.2	2008.3	2315.5	2378.7
6. Africa	NA	217.8	226.3	266.7	170.0	291.4
7. Asia	NA	452.2	644.1	812.4	416.6	550.7
8. L. America	NA	1175.5	974.1	1121.3	1028.5	1388.5
9. China	NA	122.6	795.9	1309.5	1489.8	2019.4
10. U.S.	2724.0	2330.1	1966.1	2174.4	2006.8	1680.9
Totals						
11. World	NA	2116.2	3007.0	2294.5	2060.1	2000.6
12. Non-U.S. World	NA	2009.9	3502.9	2349.3	2082.7	2126.9
13. Poor Nations	NA	546.1	735.0	959.1	828.7	1134.8
14. Rich Nations	NA	2384.1	3417.6	2521.4	2272.5	2160.0

Source: Appendix Tables III-1 and V-8.

Appendix Table IV-9
Intensity-of-Use: Primary Aluminum
(metric tons per billion $ GDP)

Region	1934-38	1951-55	1956-60	1961-65	1966-70	1971-75
1. W. Europe	892.0	1564.9	1954.1	2283.0	2686.3	3056.3
2. Japan	534.0	866.4	1848.5	2258.2	3533.6	4863.3
3. ODL	182.0	1286.9	1357.4	1803.4	2408.6	2876.2
4. U.S.S.R.	316.0	1362.9	1691.3	2106.1	2205.5	2413.3
5. E. Europe	NA	875.8	1767.9	2246.7	3027.7	3646.7
6. Africa	NA	36.7	56.6	163.2	346.2	559.2
7. Asia	NA	140.4	284.3	764.0	1332.0	1461.8
8. L. America	NA	368.9	545.0	879.3	1207.2	1656.3
9. China	NA	43.5	558.5	1033.3	1477.7	1629.5
10. U.S.	493.0	2174.2	2387.9	3002.3	3647.3	3910.6
Totals						
11. World	NA	1478.1	1778.9	2239.3	2763.2	3092.8
12. Non-U.S. World	NA	1102.9	1488.7	1892.0	2387.9	2769.5
13. Poor Nations	NA	168.7	411.8	790.5	1208.2	1461.1
14. Rich Nations	NA	1701.5	2025.0	2485.4	3031.4	3393.7

Source: Appendix Tables III-1 and V-9.

Appendix Table IV-10
Intensity-of-Use: Platinum-Group Metals
(troy ounces per billion $ GDP)

Region	1934-38*	1951-55	1956-60	1961-65	1966-70	1971-75**
1. W. Europe		388	651	676	751	698
2. Japan		411	1451	3151	3924	6847
3. ODL†		499	885	1425	1299	1480
4. U.S.S.R. and						
E. Europe		NA	NA	582	651	831
6. Africa		11	7	95	406	534
7. Asia		61	66	170	483	698
8. L. America		191	180	165	271	170
9. China†		NA	NA	95	1111	856
10. U.S.		1035	1239	1293	1500	1479
Totals						
11. World		NA	NA	906	1121	1360
12. Non-U.S. World		NA	NA	730	959	1313
13. Poor Nations		NA	NA	142	551	545
14. Rich Nations		NA	NA	1036	1219	1511

Source: Appendix Tables III-1 and V-10.

*NA

**Preliminary; regions (3)-(9) based on approximations from 1971-73 only.

†Approximate data.

Appendix Table IV-11
Intensity-of-Use: Zinc
(metric tons per billion $ GDP)

Region	1934-38	1951-55	1956-60	1961-65	1966-70	1971-75
1. W. Europe	2591.0	1908.9	2022.9	1940.8	1767.5	1660.8
2. Japan	2122.0	1901.9	1788.4	2925.6	3034.0	2612.4
3. ODL	1251.0	1672.6	1782.9	1815.8	1811.9	1724.3
4. U.S.S.R.	494.0	1109.7	1112.4	1010.6	1157.7	1347.6
5. E. Europe	NA	1390.3	1713.8	1849.8	2053.7	1995.4
6. Africa	NA	22.9	49.5	122.0	290.8	327.5
7. Asia	NA	366.6	658.3	956.2	1047.9	1041.5
8. L. America	NA	698.6	730.5	866.6	957.1	1128.5
9. China	NA	94.0	518.3	1119.0	1201.1	1323.1
10. U.S.	1966.0	1549.5	1308.0	1312.2	1265.1	1033.6
Totals						
11. World	NA	1408.1	1379.3	1439.5	1453.6	1390.6
12. Non-U.S. World	NA	1331.8	1413.3	1497.4	1533.6	1531.6
13. Poor Nations	NA	328.0	436.7	630.1	714.4	1052.0
14. Rich Nations	NA	1592.4	1549.7	1577.0	1581.1	1491.9

Source: Appendix Tables III-1 and V-11.

Appendix Table IV-12
Intensity-of-Use: Tin
(metric tons per billion $ GDP)

Region	1934-38	1951-55	1956-60	1961-65	1966-70	1971-75
1. W. Europe	242.0	139.5	135.5	112.3	83.2	73.5
2. Japan	215.0	128.0	165.7	159.4	138.0	127.1
3. ODL	122.0	113.5	106.1	98.1	81.4	64.4
4. U.S.S.R.	83.0	61.8	66.6	67.3	33.1	29.8
5. E. Europe	NA	70.6	55.5	65.6	85.2	76.6
6. Africa	NA	46.6	38.2	38.8	27.3	24.9
7. Asia	NA	60.8	63.1	52.9	51.2	37.8
8. L. America	NA	69.1	62.4	53.9	41.3	36.5
9. China	NA	33.5	72.0	156.0	129.1	100.8
10. U.S.	305.0	100.5	82.6	72.7	62.1	46.8
Totals						
11. World	NA	97.9	92.3	86.3	69.1	58.8
12. Non-U.S. World	NA	96.6	96.9	92.4	72.1	63.5
13. Poor Nations	NA	54.3	62.6	75.4	63.2	50.6
14. Rich Nations	NA	105.4	97.6	88.1	70.1	60.3

Source: Appendix Tables III-1 and V-12.

Appendix Table V-1
World Demand for Crude Steel
(million metric tons)
5-year averages

Region	1934-38	1951-55	1956-60	1961-65	1966-70	1971-75
1. W. Europe	44.6070	49.5745	76.8900	114.2540	122.9110	145.8620
2. Japan	NA	6.2450	18.9160	34.8210	51.9740	70.8510
3. ODL	NA	9.3420	12.6650	16.7470	21.6210	27.2890
4. U.S.S.R.	14.8752	34.2534	54.9434	77.4938	101.1270	128.9170
5. E. Europe	NA	22.9710	26.8770	33.2120	35.9120	45.9360
6. Africa	NA	1.2900	1.8740	2.4920	3.1190	4.8980
7. Asia	NA	3.5160	10.1550	12.2250	14.7680	29.2550
8. L. America	1.2870	5.0960	9.4810	13.6910	15.2950	24.9610
9. China	.2250	2.2334	10.4542	12.1642	15.9890	29.0170
10. U.S.	37.9664	91.0924	90.2552	105.8446	132.5042	135.3220
Totals						
11. World	NA	225.6137	312.5108	422.9446	515.2202	642.3080
12. Non-U.S. World	NA	134.5213	222.2556	317.1000	382.7160	506.9860
13. Poor Nations	NA	12.1354	31.9642	40.5722	49.1710	88.1310
14. Rich Nations	NA	213.4783	280.5466	382.3724	466.0492	554.1770

Source United Nations. *Statistical Yearbook* (annual) U.N. *The Steel Market* (annual)

Appendix Table V-2
World Demand for Iron Ore
(million metric tons iron content)
5-year averages

Region	1934-38*	1951-55	1956-60	1961-65	1966-70	1971-75
1. W. Europe		40.6229	59.7250	76.7612	86.1112	94.5120
2. Japan		2.9425	13.4690	26.9690	40.9890	52.7610
3. ODL		5.9410	9.9620	15.8120	18.5120	24.3120
4. U.S.S.R.		28.7610	42.0714	65.8848	84.1584	96.9210
5. E. Europe		6.2120	11.4540	16.5740	22.9110	26.2750
6. Africa		1.2136	1.7440	2.2910	2.8640	3.7792
7. Asia		2.1460	3.9860	5.5410	7.7450	10.0040
8. L. America		1.5224	5.4070	7.5770	10.4260	14.6980
9. China		2.1960	6.5240	11.8000	18.1674	23.2110
10. U.S.		59.5720	68.4650	71.8710	77.1726	85.4225
Totals						
11. World		151.1294	222.8074	301.0810	369.0566	431.8957
12. Non-U.S. World		91.5574	154.3424	229.2100	291.8840	346.4732
13. Poor Nations		7.0780	17.6610	27.2090	39.2021	51.6922
14. Rich Nations		144.0514	205.1464	273.8720	329.8542	380.2035

Source: National Commission on Materials Policy. U N. *The Steel Market* (annual)
*NA

Appendix Table V-3
World Demand for Nickel
(1000 metric tons)
5-year averages

Region	1934-38*	1951-55	1956-60	1961-65	1966-70	1971-75
1. W. Europe		52.70	66.20	101.30	144.82	169.60
2. Japan		4.42	9.82	23.56	63.98	97.28
3. ODL†		3.28	5.48	7.60	14.12	16.70
4. U.S.S.R., China & E. Europe		NA	57.82	105.20	119.00	159.44
6. Africa		0.12	0.26	0.90	3.72	4.42
7. Asia		0.31	0.42	1.58	1.72	3.66
8. L. America		0.36	0.68	1.18	1.94	6.74
10. U.S.		69.32	99.76	122.12	151.66	160.54
Totals						
11. World		NA	240.44	363.44	500.96	618.38
12. Non-U.S. World		NA	140.68	241.32	349.30	457.84

Source: Metallgesellschaft Aktiengesellschaft. *Metal Statistics* (annual).
*NA
†South Africa included with Africa (line 6)

Appendix Table V-4

World Demand for Manganese Ore

(1000 metric tons)

5-year averages

Region	1934-38	1951-55	1956-60	1961-65	1966-70	1971-75*
1. W. Europe	1345	1647	2288	2664	3715	4134
2. Japan	222	336	527	758	1038	1667
3. ODL	132	421	674	619	704	789
4. U.S.S.R.	1732	3297	4400	5786	5772	6420
5. E. Europe	359	705	1041	1096	1134	1157
6. Africa	122	99	169	221	308	480
7. Asia	110	180	229	669	1157	1384
8. L. America	18	180	184	673	687	1071
9. China	4	170	864	919	920	998
10. U.S.	629	1768	1755	1909	2090	1929
Totals						
11. World	4673	8803	12133	15314	17525	20030
12. Non-U.S. World	4044	7035	10378	13405	15435	18101
13. Poor Nations	254	629	1446	2483	3072	3934
14. Rich Nations	4418	8174	10625	12831	14455	16096

Source: Overseas Geological Surveys—Mineral Resource Division. *Statistical Summary of the Mineral Industry, Production, Exports and Imports* (1934-1971). U.S.B.M. *Minerals Yearbook* (1934-74). Metal Bulletin Limited.
Metal Bulletin Handbook (1969-76). United Nations *World Trade Annual and Its Supplement* (1971-74).

* Preliminary. In particular the figure for ODL (3) is uncertain due to inventory adjustments

Appendix Table V-5
World Demand for Chrome Ore
(1000 metric tons)
5-year averages

Region	1934-38	1951-55	1956-60	1961-65	1966-70	1971-75*
1. W. Europe	459	719	985	1080	1901	1873
2. Japan	34	76	251	365	753	1127
3. ODL	36	233	209	256	498	740
4. U.S.S.R.	158	320	406	485	548	750
5. E. Europe	33	181	236	352	448	744
6. Africa	4	9	13	18	33	49
7. Asia	9	30	41	52	93	184
8. L. America	9	12	16	21	57	109
9. China	NA	14	24	58	165	216
10. U.S.	388	1131	1340	1188	1260	1149
Totals						
11. World	NA	2725	3521	3875	5756	6941
12. Non-U.S. World	NA	1594	2181	2687	4496	5792
13. Poor Nations	NA	65	95	149	348	558
14. Rich Nations	1108	2660	3426	3726	5408	6383

Source: Overseas Geological Surveys. Mineral Resource Division. Statistical Summary of the Mineral Industry, Production, Exports and Imports (1934-1971). U.S.B.M. Minerals Yearbook (1934-74). Metals Bulletin Limited. Metal Bulletin Handbook (1909-76). United Nations. World Trade Annual and Its Supplement (1971-74).

* Preliminary

Appendix Table V-6
World Demand for Cobalt
(metric tons)
5-year averages

Region	1934-38*	1951-55	1956-60	1961-65	1966-70	1971-75**
1. W. Europe		2490	2523	4780	5841	6113
2. Japan		261	781	1487	3388	3941
3. ODL		491	940	1069	1175	1506
4. U.S.S.R.		423	600	932	1320	1981
5. E. Europe		435	636	885	1026	1108
6. Africa		345	498	520	652	706
7. Asia		9	30	68	142	255
8. L. America		88	73	96	238	342
9. China		16	24	46	90	200
10. U.S.		4407	4090	5046	6363	7282
Totals						
11. World		8965	10195	14929	20235	23434
12. Non-U.S. World		4558	6105	9883	13872	16152
13. Poor Nations		458	625	730	1122	1503
14. Rich Nations		8507	9570	14199	19113	21931

Source: Overseas Geological Surveys—Mineral Resource Division. *Statistical Summary of the Mineral Industry, Production, Exports and Imports* (1934-1971); U.S.B.M.. *Minerals Yearbook* (1934-74); Metal Bulletin Limited. *Metal Bulletin Handbook* (1909-76); United Nations. *World Trade Annual and Its Supplement* (1971-74).
*NA
**Preliminary.

Appendix Table V-7
World Demand for Tungsten
(metric tons)
5-year averages

Region	1934-38	1951-55	1956-60	1961-65	1966-70	1971-75*
1. W. Europe	7996	5170	6847	8456	10404	11575
2. Japan	NA	496	1120	1970	2812	2758
3. ODL	81	101	139	342	524	578
4. U.S.S.R.	782	3581	4016	5442	6205	6645
5. E. Europe	NA	1090	1610	2160	3488	3824
6. Africa	62	61	79	72	249	685
7. Asia	NA	430	565	534	857	849
8. L. America	107	562	559	281	872	1372
9. China	NA	2320	3022	3649	4805	5386
10. U.S.	2854	3699	4025	5630	6596	6510
Totals						
11. World	NA	17510	21992	28536	36812	40182
12. Non-U.S. World	NA	13811	17967	22906	30216	33672
13. Poor Nations	NA	3373	4235	4536	6783	8292
14. Rich Nations	NA	14137	17757	24000	30029	31890

Source Overseas Geological Surveys Mineral Resource Division. *Statistical Summary of the Mineral Industry, Production, Exports and Imports* (1934-1971). U.S.B.M. *Minerals Yearbook* (1934-74) Metal Bulletin Limited.
Metal Bulletin Handbook (1909-76). United Nations. *World Trade Annual and Its Supplement* (1971-74)
* Preliminary

119

Appendix Table V-8
World Demand for Refined Copper
(1000 metric tons)
5-year averages

Region	1934-38	1951-55	1956-60	1961-65	1966-70	1971-75
1. W. Europe	900.64	1142.94	1599.18	1919.38	2055.04	2421.72
2. Japan	155.02	98.30	1969.94	382.20	684.24	921.96
3. ODL	57.46	168.34	193.22	333.78	366.66	356.62
4. U.S.S.R.	181.72	386.00	520.34	728.18	727.20	1097.00
5. E. Europe	65.58	146.66	200.42	282.82	404.28	539.20
6. Africa	4.30	5.70	7.68	11.54	9.46	20.80
7. Asia	16.42	34.78	61.84	97.42	64.50	110.88
8. L. America	57.46	78.58	84.30	125.26	151.56	278.08
9. China	NA	7.60	69.40	110.00	160.00	290.00
10. U.S.	581.38	1298.12	1258.64	1681.26	1891.06	1886.08
Totals						
11. World	NA	3367.02	5964.96	5671.84	6514.00	7922.71
12. Non-U.S. World	NA	2068.90	4706.32	3990.58	4622.94	6036.62
13. Poor Nations	NA	126.66	223.22	344.22	385.52	699.77
14. Rich Nations	1941.80	3240.36	5741.74	5327.62	6128.48	7222.94

Source Metallgesellschaft Aktiengesellschaft. *Metal Statistics* (annual)

Appendix Table V-9
World Demand for Primary Aluminum
(1000 metric tons)
5-year averages

Region	1934-38	1951-55	1956-60	1961-65	1966-70	1971-75
1. W. Europe	242.92	608.96	942.64	1380.98	2063.02	2861.62
2. Japan	19.46	38.04	118.72	227.80	604.75	1253.66
3. ODL	6.58	93.62	118.72	200.40	349.16	527.70
4. U.S.S.R.	36.90	286.00	494.52	804.60	1192.72	1490.00
5. E. Europe	5.46	75.68	200.50	316.40	528.62	826.62
6. Africa	0.10	0.96	1.92	7.06	19.26	39.92
7. Asia	1.26	10.80	27.29	91.62	206.21	294.34
8. L. America	1.28	24.66	47.16	98.22	177.90	332.72
9. China	NA	2.70	48.70	86.80	158.70	234.00
10. U.S.	105.12	1211.25	1528.66	2321.48	3436.90	4388.10
Totals						
11. World	NA	2351.77	3528.83	5535.36	8737.24	12248.69
12. Non-U.S. World	NA	1140.42	2000.17	3213.88	5300.34	7860.59
13. Poor Nations	NA	39.12	125.07	283.70	562.07	900.98
14. Rich Nations	416.44	2312.56	3403.76	5251.66	8175.17	11347.71

Source: Metalgessellschaft Aktiengesellschaft. *Metal Statistics* (annual)

121

Appendix Table V-10

World Demand for the Platinum-Group

(1000 troy ounces)
5-year averages

Region	1934-38*	1951-55	1956-60	1961-65	1966-70	1971-75**
1. W. Europe	151.0		314.2	408.9	576.2	653.2
2. Japan	18.0		93.2	317.9	671.6	1765.1
3. ODL†	36.3		77.4	158.2	188.3	271.7
4. U.S.S.R. & E. Europe	NA		NA	304.6	436.7	701.7
6. Africa	0.3		0.2	4.1	22.6	38.2
7. Asia	4.7		6.4	20.4	74.8	140.7
8. L. America	12.7		15.5	18.4	39.8	34.0
9. China†	NA		NA	8.0	119.3	123.0
10. U.S.	576.6		793.2	999.5	1413.5	1659.6
Totals						
11. World	NA		NA	2240.0	3542.8	5387.2
12. Non-U.S. World	NA		NA	1240.5	2129.3	3727.6
13. Poor Nations	NA		NA	50.9	256.5	335.9
14. Rich Nations	NA		NA	2189.1	3286.7	5051.3

Source: *Statistical Summary of the Mineral Industry* (1951-1971); U.S.B.M.. *Minerals Yearbook* (1951-1971). *Minerals Yearbook* (1951-1974); Overseas Geological Surveys   Mineral Resources Division *Statistical Summary of the Mineral Industry. Production, Exports and Imports* (1951-1971); U.S B M . *Minerals Yearbook* (annual).

* NA

** Preliminary; in particular regions (3)-(9) based on 1971-73 approximations.

†Approximate data.

Appendix Table V-11
World Demand for Zinc
(1000 metric tons)
5-year averages

Region	1934-38	1951-55	1956-60	1961-65	1966-70	1971-75
1. W. Europe	705.56	742.82	975.84	1173.98	1357.38	1555.01
2. Japan	77.36	83.50	114.86	295.12	519.24	673.42
3. ODL	45.20	121.68	153.94	201.78	262.66	316.40
4. U.S.S.R.	57.82	232.86	325.26	386.08	574.00	832.12
5. E. Europe	66.72	120.14	194.36	260.50	358.56	452.30
6. Africa	0.41	0.60	1.68	5.28	16.18	24.48
7. Asia	25.62	28.20	63.20	114.66	162.22	209.73
8. L. America	13.62	46.70	63.22	96.80	141.04	226.02
9. China	NA	5.80	45.21	94.04	129.41	190.01
10. U.S.	419.54	863.26	837.32	1014.66	1192.16	1159.82
Totals						
11. World	NA	2240.34	2736.20	3558.26	4596.34	5506.26
12. Non-U.S. World	NA	1377.08	1898.88	2543.60	3404.18	4346.21
13. Poor Nations	NA	76.08	132.62	226.14	332.34	649.10
14. Rich Nations	1372.20	2164.26	2603.58	3332.12	4264.00	4989.93

Source: Metallgesellschaft Aktiengesellschaft. *Metal Statistics* (annual)

Appendix Table V-12
World Demand for Tin
(1000 metric tons)
5-year averages

Region	1934-38	1951-55	1956-60	1961-65	1966-70	1971-75
1. W. Europe	65.80	54.30	65.36	67.94	63.90	68.84
2. Japan	7.92	5.62	10.64	16.08	23.62	32.76
3. ODL	4.40	8.26	9.28	10.90	11.80	11.82
4. U.S.S.R.	9.72	12.96	19.48	25.70	16.40	18.40
5. E. Europe	2.72	6.10	6.30	9.24	14.88	17.14
6. Africa	1.18	1.22	1.34	1.68	1.52	1.78
7. Asia	4.70	4.68	6.06	6.34	7.92	7.62
8. L. America	2.80	4.62	5.40	6.02	6.08	7.32
9. China	2.50	2.08	6.28	13.10	13.86	14.48
10. U.S.	65.00	55.98	52.90	56.22	58.48	52.56
Totals						
11. World	166.74	155.82	183.04	213.22	218.46	232.72
12. Non-U.S. World	101.74	99.84	130.14	157.00	159.98	180.16
13. Poor Nations	11.18	12.60	19.08	27.14	29.38	31.20
14. Rich Nations	155.56	143.22	163.96	186.08	189.07	201.52

Source: Metallgesellschaft Aktiengesellschaft. *Metal Statistics* (annual).

124

Bibliography

American Metals Market. *Metal Statistics*. New York: Fairchild Publication, annual.

Banks, Ferdinand. *The World Copper Market: An Economic Analysis*. Cambridge, Mass.: Ballinger Publishing Company, 1974.

Barbier, Claude. *The Economics of Tungsten*. London: Metal Bulletin Books Limited, 1971.

Bergson, Abram. *Soviet National Income and Product in 1937*. New York: Columbia University Press, 1953.

Bohm, Peter. *Pricing of Copper in International Trade*. Stockholm: Stockholm School of Economics, 1968.

Brooks, D.B. and Andrews, P.W. "Mineral Resources, Economic Growth and World Population." *Science*, 5 July 1974, pp 13-19.

Brown, Martin and Butler, John. *The Production, Marketing and Consumption of Copper and Aluminum*. New York: Praeger, 1968.

Burrows, James C. *Tungsten: An Industry Analysis*. Lexington, Mass: Lexington Books, 1971.

Cockerill, Anthony and Silberston, Aubrey. *The Steel Industry: International Comparisons of Industrial Structure and Performance*. London: Cambridge University Press, 1974.

Dowsing, R. "Zinc from Protective Coating to Formed Superplastics." *Metals and Materials*, March 1976.

Edison Electric Institute. Committee on Economic Growth, Pricing and Energy Use. *Economic Growth in the Future: The Growth Debate, in National and Global Perspective*. New York: McGraw-Hill Book Company, 1976.

Elliot-James, M.F. *Long-Term Projections of Primary Metals Markets*. New York: The Conference Board, 1972.

Garzouzi, Eva. *Economic Growth and Development: The Less Developed Countries*. New York: Vantage Press, 1972.

Greene, David. *Steel and Economic Development: Capital-Output Ratios in Three Latin American Steel Plants*. East Lansing, Mich: Graduate School of Business Administration, Michigan State University, 1967.

Hogan, William. *The 1970s: Critical Years for Steel*. Lexington, Mass: Lexington Books, 1972.

International Bank for Reconstruction and Development. *World Bank Atlas*. Washington: IBRD, 1977.

International Iron and Steel Institute, Committee on Economic Studies. *Projection 85: World Steel Demand*. Brussels, March 1972.

Kawahito, Kiyoshi. *The Japanese Steel Industry*. New York: Praeger, 1972.

Kellogg, Herbert. "Energy and Primary Materials." *Engineering and Mining Journal*, Vol. 178, No. 4 (April 1977).

Kuznets, Simon. *Modern Economic Growth*. New Haven: Yale University Press, 1966.

Landsberg, Hans, Fischman, Leonard and Fisher, Joseph. *Resources in America's Future: Patterns of Requirements and Availabilities 1960-2000*. Baltimore: Johns Hopkins Press, 1963.

Landsberg, Hans H. "Materials: Some Recent Trends and Issues." *Science*, 20 February 1976, pp 637-41.

Leontief, Wassily et al. *The Future of the World Economy*. New York: Oxford University Press, 1977.

Liu, Ta-chung. *China's National Income 1931-36: An Exploratory Study*. Washington: Brookings Institution, 1946.

Liu, Ta-chung and Yeh, Kung-chia. *The Economy of the Chinese Mainland: National Income and Economic Development*. Santa Monica: RAND Corporation, 1963.

Lorimer, Frank. *The Population of the Soviet Union: History and Prospects*. Geneva: League of Nations, 1946.

Malenbaum, Wilfred. *Modern India's Economy*. Columbus, Ohio: Charles E. Merrill Publishing Company, 1971.

Malenbaum, Wilfred, et al. *Materials Requirements in the United States and Abroad in the Year 2000*. Washington: National Commission on Materials Policy, 1973.

Manners, Gerald. *The Changing World Market for Iron Ore 1950-1980*. Baltimore: Johns Hopkins Press, 1971.

Meadows, Dennis, et al. *The Limits to Growth*. A Report for The Club of Rome's Project on the Predicament of Mankind. New York: Universe Books, 1972.

Metal Bulletin Limited. *Metal Bulletin Handbook*. London: Metal Bulletin Limited, annual.

Metallgesselschaft Aktiengesellschaft. *Metal Statistics*. Frankfurt-Am-Main: Metallgesselschaft a.g., annual.

National Academy of Sciences. *Mineral Resources and the Environment*. Washington: U.S. Government Printing Office, 1975.

National Commission on Materials Policy. *Material Needs and the Environment Today and Tomorrow*. Washington: U.S. Government Printing Office, 1973.

National Council of Applied Economic Research. *Demand for Steel in 1975 and 1980*. New Delhi: National Council for Applied Economic Research, 1971.

North Atlantic Treaty Organization Science Committee Study Group, NATO Scientific Affairs Division. *Rational Use of Potentially Scarce Metals.* Brussels: NATO, 1976.

Overseas Geological Survey, Mineral Resources Division. *Statistical Summary of the Mineral Industry, Production, Exports and Imports.* London: Her Majesty's Stationary Office, annual.

Radcliffe, S.V. "World Changes and Chances: Some New Perspectives for Materials." *Science,* 20 February 1976, pp. 700-07.

Ridker, Ronald G. (ed.). *Changing Resource Problems of the Fourth World.* Washington: Resources for the Future, 1976.

    Population, Resources and the Environment. A Report to the U.S. Commission on Population Growth and the American Future. Washington: U.S. Government Printing Office, 1972.

Ruist, E. et al. *Forecasting Steel Consumption.* Paris: OECD, 1974.

Seidman, Ann (ed.). *Natural Resources and National Welfare: The Case of Copper.* New York: Praeger, 1972.

United Nations Conference on Trade and Development. *Commodity Problems and Policies.* Report by UNCTAD Secretariat, Third Session, Santiago, Chile, April 1972.

United Nations, Department of Economic Affairs. *A Study of the Iron and Steel Industry in Latin America.* New York: United Nations, 1954.

    Steel Production and Consumption Trends in Europe and the World. Geneva: United Nations, 1952.

United Nations, Department of Economic and Social Affairs. *Demographic Yearbook.* New York: United Nations, annual.

    Population by Sex and Age for Regions and Countries, 1950-2000, As Assessed in 1973. New York: United Nations, 1976.

    Statistical Yearbook. New York: United Nations, annual.

    World Economic Survey 1975: Fluctuations and Developments in the World Economy. New York: United Nations, 1976.

    The World Population Situation in 1970-1975 and its Long-Range Implications. New York: United Nations, 1974.

    World Population Prospects As Assessed in 1968. Population Studies No. 53. New York: United Nations, 1973.

    World Population Prospects As Assessed in 1973. Population Studies, No. 60. New York: United Nations, 1977.

    Yearbook of National Accounts Statistics. New York: United Nations, annual.

United Nations, Economic Commission for Europe. *Steel and Its Alternatives.* Geneva: United Nations, 1956.

    The European Steel Market in 1964. New York: United Nations, 1964.

    The Steel Market in 1968. New York: United Nations, 1969.

    The Steel Market in 1976. New York: United Nations, 1977.

    The World Market for Iron Ore. New York: United Nations, 1968.

    World Trade in Steel and Steel Demand in Developing Countries. New York: United Nations, 1968.

United Nations Industrial Development Organization. *Industrialization of Developing Countries: Problems and Prospects—The Iron and Steel Industry.* Monographs on Industrial Development. New York: United Nations, 1969.

    Industrialization of Developing Countries: Problems and Prospects—The Non-Ferrous Metals Industry. Monographs on Industrial Development. New York: United Nations, 1969.

    The Iron and Steel Industry in Developing Countries. New York: United Nations, 1974.

United States, Central Intelligence Agency. *Handbook of Economic Statistics, 1975.* Washington, 1976.

United States Congress, Joint Economic Committee. *New Directions in the Soviet Economy.* Washington: U.S. Government Printing Office, 1966.

    People's Republic of China: An Economic Assessment. Washington: U.S. Government Printing Office, 1972.

    Soviet Economic Prospects for the Seventies. Washington: U.S. Government Printing Office, 1973.

United States, Department of Commerce, Bureau of International Economic Policy and Research. *International Economic Indicators and Competitive Trends.* Washington: U.S. Government Printing Office, 1975.

United States, Department of the Interior, Bureau of Mines. *Mineral Facts and Problems.* Washington: U.S. Government Printing Office.

    Minerals Yearbook. Washington: U.S. Government Printing Office, annual.

United States, Department of State, Bureau of Intelligence and Research. *The Planetary Product in 1972: Systems in Disarray.* Washington, 1973.

Warren, Kenneth. *World Steel: An Economic Geography.* New York: Crane, Russell and Co., 1975.

Zinc Institute. *U.S. Annual Zinc Review.* New York: Zinc Institute, annual.

    Why Zinc? New York: Zinc Institute, 1970.

DATE DUE

5 Feb 82			